Owning Up

Owning Up

The 14 Questions Every Board Member Needs to Ask

Ram Charan

JOSSEY-BASS
A Wiley Imprint
www.josseybass.com

Published by Jossey-Bass
A Wiley Imprint
989 Market Street, San Francisco, CA 94103-1741—www.josseybass.com

Jossey-Bass books and products are available through most bookstores. To contact Jossey-Bass
directly call our Customer Care Department within the U.S. at 800-956-7739, outside the
U.S. at 317-572-3986, or fax 317-572-4002.

Jossey-Bass also publishes its books in a variety of electronic formats. Some content that appears
in print may not be available in electronic books.

Library of Congress cataloging-in-publication data has been applied for.

ISBN 978-0-470-39767-1

Printed in the United States of America
FIRST EDITION
HB Printing   10 9 8 7 6 5 4 3 2 1

Contents

Foreword

Societal demands and expectations have caused a tectonic shift in the role of the board. The first shock was felt in 1993 when the board of General Motors broke the mold and forced out a CEO who was not performing. Since then, boards in the U.S. and U.K. have been prodded and pleaded with to take a more active role, and in recent years, indeed they have. Expectations for boards were raised further with the passage of Sarbanes-Oxley in 2002, which erased any doubt that boards must ensure that their companies' fiscal houses are in order.

Now boards find themselves thrust into the spotlight yet again and challenged to do even more. In the midst of the near total breakdown of the global financial system, shareholders and other constituencies are looking to boards to help their companies find a safe place to land. Even good companies with AAA ratings have been swept up in the tsunami. Surely the board can pick up and patch up what the CEO cannot, the thinking goes. Directors have scrambled to meet this newest demand and fill the void, adjusting their schedules and their priorities and approaching their board work with increased rigor.

With this immense pressure and the sudden surge of engagement by some boards, the break from the past is now complete. Boards are no longer waiting for issues to come their way. They are trying to identify them early and to get ahead of them. This new set of circumstances creates new dynamics between the board and management, between the board and external constituencies, and among the independent directors.

No wonder questions are arising in boardrooms nationwide. As if the business issues were not challenging enough, boards are also trying to reinvent their work on the fly.

Fortunately, there are answers. In this succinct and timely book, Ram Charan takes on the questions that are top of mind among directors. A life-long student of corporate governance, advisor to CEOs and corporate boards, and director serving on three boards himself, Ram has an unparalleled experience base from which to provide the answers. He has observed many boards in action and won the confidence of many highly respected directors. He has watched as boards have worked to adjust to the new developments in corporate governance. What he has found, and catalogues so well in this book, is a number of cutting edge practices that are exactly right for the times.

In his inimitable style, Ram provides advice that is both wise and practical. He takes into account the realities of human behavior and group dynamics as well as the ambiguities of running a business in today's environment. He sees issues in their entirety yet clarifies the way forward. And he does not mask his views about where boards need to take a stronger stance.

Directors, CEOs, senior executives, and anyone else who has a stake in the quality of corporate governance will be interested in the sound advice and insights found here. I encourage you to keep reading, and learning, and making a positive difference to the companies on whose boards you serve.

Jack Krol
Former chairman and CEO, DuPont
Director, Tyco International, Ltd.
January 2009

What Boards Need Now

The meltdown in the global financial system in 2007–8 followed by a deep and probably long economic downturn sent a wake-up call to corporate boards. Directors are energized to roll up their sleeves and get to work, yet they have more questions and anxiety than ever.

Their companies are facing unprecedented challenges. Cash vulnerabilities at many companies are revealed daily, and lack of liquidity is in some cases turning into insolvency. In many industries demand has fallen off a cliff. For example, demand for automobiles and parts plunged by more than 30 percent in fewer than 90 days. As recently as late last year analysts and investors were recommending that companies should use cash to buy back shares, and some directors wholeheartedly agreed, even encouraging management to do so more aggressively. One director, chairman of his board's finance committee, recently remarked, "Why didn't I move faster to suggest that management ignore the analysts and reverse that decision?" Urgency has taken hold. In September–October 2008, some boards met more than six times on very short notice—and with full attendance.

The business landscape has changed. The game has changed. What boards do needs to change as well. The change is this: *Boards need to own up to their accountability for the performance of the corporation.* In the past, employees, shareholders, and the press looked to the CEO to ensure that the corporation performed well. Now they have also begun to look to you, the board, to be the leader. You need to own up to this accountability for the business. As one director put it, "Boards can make a company or break a company."

The financial meltdown has revealed how boards of Wall Street firms and some financial institutions outside the United States have failed in their accountability. Boards are institutions with public constituencies. The public and the watchdogs can differentiate a legitimate explanation (no one could have seen the financial tsunami coming, and besides, everyone is in the same boat) from poor performance. Most directors care about their reputation. It is no fun to be forced to resign from the board through the pressure of public exposure, even though you did nothing illegal.

The role of the board has changed forever. *"Governance" now means leadership,* not just over-the-shoulder monitoring and passive approvals. Boards must fiercely guard their companies against threats of rapid decline and sudden demise, while at the same time helping management seize the opportunities that tumultuous change presents but are hard to see in the daily fray of running the business. The board that does both turns governance into a competitive advantage.

In my research for this book I have talked one on one with many directors and closely observed almost fifty in the boardroom. I found a very positive and healthy dose of realism. They have begun to search for what works and what does not work. They want to do what is right, but they know they cannot sustain the pace of six short-notice meetings in sixty days and expect full attendance. *Directors need to reinvent the content of their work and their modus operandi.* They need answers to their many questions.

My observation of boards and interviews with many of you inspired this book. I have designed it to directly and concisely address the burning contemporary issues directors and their boards are wrestling with. The fourteen questions that follow are the ones that I hear from directors most often. My responses to them draw on my forty years of experience advising boards as well as observations of best practices I have seen emerging in recent months and even weeks. The three boards I serve on have also allowed me to see what works and does not work.

The recommendations in this book are meant to be practical and to get to the heart of the unique issues boards are facing now. I recommend that every director, particularly new directors, read the book in its entirety to fully grasp how boards can own up. But I've also organized the book so you can quickly access the particular questions or issues that are most urgent for you.

It's my hope that you and your colleagues will use the content of this book to help your board truly **own up** to the new role society is demanding of you. As the business environment continues to be volatile, the specific challenges may shift, but there will be no return to board seats as comfortable, prestigious positions to retire to. Directors must face the challenges head on and see to it that their managements do the same.

What is here is a work in progress; it will never be complete. I welcome the chance to learn from you as I continue to gather the messy real-life data that is the foundation of my observational research. Your reading may stimulate more questions. I'd be honored to hear them from you. I'll do my best to return an e-mail from every director and CEO who contacts me at www .ram-charan.com.

Owning Up

Question 1.

IS OUR BOARD COMPOSITION RIGHT FOR THE CHALLENGE?

The role of the board has unmistakably transitioned from passive governance to active leadership with a delicate balance of avoiding micromanaging. It's leadership as a group, not leadership by an appointed person. This group needs the right composition to succeed, and that composition will have to change, sometimes abruptly, as conditions do. With the right composition, a board can create value; with the wrong or inappropriate composition, it can easily destroy value.

In April 2008, Citigroup added an extraordinary job posting to its website, seeking individuals with "a particular emphasis on expertise in finance and investments." What made the post so unusual were the positions Citigroup was trying to fill: directors. It took $18 billion in write-downs in the fourth quarter of 2007 and capital infusions of over $20 billion for the largest bank in the world to realize its board lacked finance and investment know-how.

The financial services meltdown in the fall of 2008 exposed the stark reality that Citigroup was not an isolated case of a board lacking the crucial expertise it needed to act like an owner. As we now see all too clearly, Bear Stearns and a host of boards in the financial services industry did not have enough depth of knowledge or experience to ensure their companies stayed on track. It has been a devastating lesson for those companies, some of which are now extinct.

But don't be fooled into thinking it's them, not us. The lesson applies beyond financial services to all boards: directors as a group must have the specific skills and perspectives needed to carry out their responsibilities. These skills must match the needs of the company in its current macro-economic and competitive context, and they must evolve with the times.

Too many boards don't know what they're missing until it's too late. A great board grabs hold of its own composition and does *succession planning* for the board itself. It objectively examines the membership of the board to ensure it has the skills that are needed, periodically asking, "If we owned this business, what expertise would we need to govern it? And how will that change in the next few years?"

How Do We Figure Out What Our Board Needs?

Functional expertise—accounting, marketing, and technology, for example—or CEO experience are crucial and expected. But you can't just run through a generic checklist to figure out what your board needs. Boards have to ensure their members have the specific expertise to ask the right questions to make a good CEO better, to affect the company's choice of short- and long-term goals, to judge and approve the strategy, and to maintain relationships with stakeholders like activists and regulators. For instance, a company that is planning a footprint in the Chinese market will benefit from having at least one board member who is an expert on the political workings of China and its culture.

Few boards consider the expertise they need with such *clarity* and *specificity*. In 2002, the collective lack of boards' audit abilities so appalled regulators that Congress rushed through the Sarbanes-Oxley Act, which included the requirement that every board have accounting expertise. Uncertainty over how it would be interpreted and implemented prevailed for many CEOs and CFOs, who now had to personally sign off on financial statements. And it set off a rush of searches for new directors who qualified as accounting experts under the new rules.

General Electric was ahead of the curve. A year earlier, the GE board, along with CEO Jeff Immelt, anticipated the growing importance of board accounting expertise and recruited Bob Swieringa, a professor of accounting who had also served as chairman of the Financial Accounting Standards Board. Swieringa's command of the evolving vagaries of financial reporting was a vital addition to the board's expertise—and the GE board was ready for Sarbanes-Oxley before its rules came into force.

Similarly, a Fortune 500 company in a low-margin, highly capital-intensive business, in which logistics is the third highest cost component, had a high-powered board of retired CEOs and CFOs but lacked expertise to add value in the logistics area. They actively recruited a director who had a CEO viewpoint and also had deep knowledge of global logistics. That director has spent a lot of time getting to know the managers and processes involved in the supply chain, and now asks questions and makes suggestions the other directors would not have thought of.

Initially, management was apprehensive about whether the director would micromanage, as might be the case any time a director with deep expertise in a subject or domain joins a board. But he was not intrusive. He handled himself as a coach and helped management see a different view. This effort resulted in better cash flow and cost productivity in logistics. Management has come to regard him as a highly valuable resource. His inclusion has made a huge difference in the board's ability to monitor operations and add value. That board also continues to discuss what expertise it should look for in future directors.

The governance committee plays a central role. It should help the board do the careful thinking needed to pinpoint and anticipate future needs based on how the business and the external environment are changing. Directors should think not only defensively—on risk and compliance—but also offensively, about areas where a board must add value. It takes time to search for and vet candidates, so the board should start looking for such director candidates right away and plan three to five years ahead.

Of course, you have to understand what skills you already have in order to figure out what skills you need. Hellene Runtagh, director of Lincoln Electric, Harman International, and NeuStar, describes a successful practice: "Some of my boards employ a simple but effective process. They have each board member complete a skill assessment matrix. They then aggregate this input and get a good overview of where the board is strong, as well as where they would benefit from additional talent. A board may find they are light on consumer industry experience, technology, or strategic skills. The board can then target those weaknesses as they select new board candidates. The Nominating and Corporate Governance Committee usually owns this process." Some other boards use this same idea of a skills matrix (see Table 1.1 at the end of the chapter). The governance committee chair or Lead Director can ensure that the matrix accurately reflects each director's skills, expertise, and experience.

The process is important because a board full of generalists is not good enough anymore. Boards still need generalists, directors who have a broad perspective on the business, but they also need domain expertise, be it in IT, logistics, or Indian culture. True, sometimes the need for domain expertise is only temporary, in which case a consultant could provide advice to the board. But if it's a critical, ongoing issue, a director must bring that expertise to the board.

Consider what new skills will be needed as times change. It could be new knowledge—of structured credit, global logistics, or accounting standards. Or it could be specific experiences, like a turnaround or cross-industry disruption. The combination of Google's ascendance and Apple's ubiquitous iPod digital music player have completely rewritten the rules for different parts of the media industry, such as music labels, newspapers, television networks, and ad agencies. In one of those sectors, a board with an ownership viewpoint might consider adding someone with insights on rapidly shifting alliances with part-ners in their ecosystem, or someone with experience acquiring and integrating companies such as social networking startups that embody the new media landscape. One respected newspa-per chain is seeking directors who understand the technologies that are driving cross-industry disruptions in that business.

The knowledge of talent evaluation and compensation that a human resources professional brings is especially important for some boards. Deep understanding of capital markets, IT, logis-tics, consumer behavior, retailing, innovation processes, or how policy is evolving might be important for others. So, too, might deep knowledge of the business and political climate in a region or a country.

You also need to find the right balance among those skills, which a skills assessment matrix helps you see holistically. Most directors have a particular expertise or orientation—be it finance, branding, or manufacturing—that they bring to the dialogue. Every board benefits from a diversity of perspectives. Too many directors with the same orientation can skew boardroom dialogue, even bogging down in minutiae as they talk among themselves.

Group discussions often gravitate toward certain *bents*. For instance, a board that has several vocal directors with deep oper-ating experience and limited exposure to strategy naturally skews toward productivity or cost cutting and could neglect other fun-damental areas requiring investments, areas like innovation and future market development. A board with an overly domestic orientation might miss out on asking vital questions about the global context, such as what global drivers affect currency volatil-ity and inputs like commodity prices. Thus, a balance of skills and expertise is needed so that a board does not develop too strong a bent in a single area. Boards have to be conscious of their bent and seek new directors who can keep it balanced.

The governance committee needs to be observant and *reflect upon the bent that emerges* in board or committee meet-ings. It only takes one or two members who are powerful or personable to influence the bent. It's a natural phenomenon of any group.

Given the surprises that any corporation can face, a board might even consider ensuring it has directors who can quickly take an interim corporate leadership role if the executive team falters badly. The fallout from the subprime mortgage debacle drove the boards of several banks and financial services firms to take interim leadership positions. It's not an ideal circumstance, but boards need to be prepared for virtually any possible eventuality.

How Do We Get the Right People for the Job?

Candidates need to be assessed not only for their skills and experiences, but also for how their personalities gel with the other directors. Different backgrounds will lead to different questions and points of view, but directors must be able to express their views without offending others or shutting down debate. They must also be willing to be influenced by others if the board is to get anything done.

There are a couple of things to watch out for. As J.P. Millon, a director of CVS Caremark, Cypress Bioscience, and InfuSystem, for example, says: "When you have eight to twelve people around a table, group dynamics and chemistry are fundamental. You don't want two extremes: first, the hyper-interventionist and disruptive person who because you say one thing is going to say exactly the contrary; second, somebody who never opens their mouth."

A few other personality traits are generally a negative to the group dynamic. Some people are too narrow in their thinking: they can't get away from talking about their bent. Others are too controlling: they are so used to being in charge that they unconsciously begin to assert power in the boardroom and put the management team on the defensive.

But the biggest red flag is a big ego; I remember how a search consultant was told by a governance committee chair why a person on his list would be unsuitable for that board because the potential director wouldn't be able to contain his ego in the boardroom. Successful people have sizable egos, but an egomaniac will almost certainly destroy boardroom dynamics.

On the other hand, some personality traits are indicators that a director could make great contributions. For example, does a director have the humility to invite a counterpoint in a manner that is constructive and not argumentative? Will she put herself in the company's shoes and not just expound on her own successes? Will he have the courage to engage in debate with a fellow director or the CEO? Will she have the temperament to make her point and be willing to accept that not all her fellow directors will agree with it or even be willing to debate it? Will she have the inner humility to invite opposite viewpoints and be willing to change her mind?

Appearances can be misleading. Directors should have the ability to speak up, for example. Yet I would take a quiet director who spoke infrequently but with great wisdom and authority over a well-spoken director with a compulsion to talk. I observed one board meeting in which one director spoke probably only three times. But when he said something, it was always a powerful observation or an eye-opening question. Other board members are all ears to this director's discourse.

Success or failure as a business leader is not necessarily a telling indicator, either, of whether that person will become an effective director. I met one person who had been forced out of his job as CEO but was a great director on a different company's board. He's a powerful thinker who was humble and articulate; he just couldn't execute when he held the chief executive's role.

Getting at those personality traits takes time. Governance committees might be accustomed to interviewing candidates over dinner and doing background checks to ensure compatibility. Those can be revealing, especially if the right questions are asked and the interviewer is a keen listener. In one case, the governance committee chair asked a director candidate to give an example of how she had helped the CEO of another board she sat on. She said she had recalculated the cost of capital. She was proud that through her persistence, she had been able to get the CFO to change the cost of capital from 7.2 to 8.2 percent. The governance committee chair had served on many boards, and during this interview he sensed that she might be a nit-picker and probably lacked the broad strategic thinking the board was looking for. The more the chairman continued to ask questions, the more he became convinced that she did not have the altitude of thinking his board was looking for.

Standard reference checking is not enough. Governance committees must make the commitment to vigorously check a candidate's references by talking to other people in the board's own social and professional networks.

You'd be surprised what turns up. Asking questions about a potential candidate such as whether he or she can disagree without being disagreeable, pushing a personal agenda forward, or feeling the need to show off their knowledge in a narrow area of expertise goes a long way toward uncovering a candidate's true colors. "Somebody who might seem easygoing and personable in the interviews," says Millon, "could be described as being pretty disruptive in interactions with a group." That's somebody you don't want on your board, regardless of their skill or expertise.

What Does the Board Succession Process Look Like?

If finding the right directors sounds like a lot of work, consider what it takes to construct a board from whole cloth. That's what Jack Krol did as Lead Director of the Tyco International board (the post–Dennis Kozlowski Tyco, by the way) when he built new boards for spin-outs Covidien and Tyco Electronics. That meant identifying and selecting twenty directors in six months and ensuring they would provide the kind of effective governance needed to restore credibility—an intense, pressure-cooker version of the board succession process. His approach is instructive for every board.

The traditional approach would have been either to let the CEO nominate a few of his or her trusted peers and then let those peers bring in a few directors from their cliques or to get a head-hunter to bring a full slate to him. And while those approaches might have produced lists of smart and experienced individuals, they would not have resulted in high-functioning groups.

Krol took a different and more time-consuming course. He was very attuned to how personalities would combine to yield the most effective CEO/board relationship and group dynamic. So he dedicated himself to interviewing, checking references, and ensuring that the mix of both skills and personalities was appropriate.

The CEO works closely with the board, so it stands to reason that he or she would need to be comfortable with the individuals involved. So Krol talked with Tyco International's CEO and chair, Ed Breen, about what they wanted for their new boards, in terms of background, expertise, and types of personalities. He also involved the incoming CEOs of the spin-offs, both of whom were divisional heads at Tyco International. Together, they constructed a matrix of criteria against which potential directors could be *viewed as a group*. There was quite a bit of up-front work before any candidates were considered. And the CEO was kept apprised throughout the process.

Using a search firm to come up with a list of candidates was important at this point. "It used to be that the CEO selected his or her buddies [for the board]," says Krol. "What we've got to watch for now is that the Lead Director or nonexecutive chair doesn't select his or her buddies. We don't want to transfer the buddy system from the CEO to the nonexecutive chair or Lead Director. We need to find the best people and the best mix, and make sure they're independent, so we use a third party to come up with the candidate list for us."

On other boards, I've seen four or five directors who worked together in some past capacity form cliques because of their particular bent and comfort level working together. At times, these cliques can unintentionally evolve into a shadow board. They often begin to draw more attention from management and disrupt the functioning of the full board. To minimize that risk, it's a good idea to reach beyond personal networks to find candidates.

In Krol's case, there were twenty positions to fill, so a search firm was essential. One note on using search firms: it can be a tricky business using a large search firm that is conducting simultaneous searches. How will the firm balance among its clients when a candidate emerges with the right skills and experiences for more than one active search? The governance committee and the search firm should talk through potential conflicts before they emerge.

Boards have to work closely with their search firms to personally vet candidates. They can't fall into the trap of deferring too much of the process to the headhunter. As candidates emerged, Krol used references to personally test each individual's personal make-up and character. "A lot of times, the people that I talked to had experiences with [the candidate] on another board," Krol says. "That was very important because they could tell me what the personality of the person was like. 'Were they just sitting there and saying nothing?' 'Were they antagonistic?' 'How did they make suggestions to the board?' 'Were they a good listener?' 'Did the candidate push the board's effectiveness and dialogue forward?' 'Did the person help crystallize the important issues?' Those things are important in terms of what your relationship is going to be with your other directors and with management." He had to rule out many people after these interviews, including one candidate who was imminently qualified on paper and had a great reputation as a leader but was antagonistic toward the CEO on other boards he sat on. Krol and the search firm were in constant contact as new candidates emerged and were assessed.

The references had to come from individuals within personal social networks—that feedback is the most candid and frank you can get. The more trusted the individual the better. "There's always somebody that I knew well and so I could have a confidential conversation with them," Krol says. "You'd be surprised how much comes out just by asking them to talk. And you should go to at least two people when you're doing this, because you never know when somebody has a bias that might be unfair."

In the end, Covidien and Tyco Electronics both got strong, independent boards with a range of expertise, effective leaders, and cohesive group dynamics. To be clear, I'm one of the directors on the Tyco Electronics board and a member of its governance committee. I can genuinely say that board is among the highest-functioning boards I've observed. In less than ten months and fewer than five board meetings, the camaraderie of the directors is palpable and the discussion gets right to the critical issues and has, in the view of the CEO, added value. This information is based in part on feedback from management to the board about the board's functioning and contribution.

Although spin-outs and other events that call for new boards are not that uncommon, Krol's challenge was not something that most boards experience. Still, the steps he took are an accelerated version of what every board must do: treat board succession as a process, identify the board's needs, plan several years ahead, vet candidates through social networks over time, and be diligent in assessing candidates for their fit in terms of experience, expertise, and personality.

The Governance Committee's Pivotal Role in Board Succession

Organizing board succession is one of the central responsibilities of the governance committee and it should be part of its charter. It must take this role very seriously; if the composition of the board is not appropriate, it is a failure of the committee. The board must empower the committee to *actively shape* the board composition.

In many cases, the CEO still has a lot of influence over the selection of directors, points out Roger Kenny, president of Boardroom Consultants. But if the board is to grasp the reins of governance, the governance committee and not the CEO must have the ultimate say in director nomination.

Ever since Sarbanes-Oxley, companies have complained about the lack of availability of good directors. Many sitting CEOs, for example, have reduced the number of boards on which they sit to just two, and some sit on no boards but their own.

Qualified people are out there, however, if a board expands its search. Boards could expand their radar to consider people who are not necessarily CEOs and CFOs today but have the potential to be or have other vital experiences. That logistics expert I mentioned earlier has a military leadership background. Do not hesitate to identify people who meet your criteria and are first-time directors. In fact, research shows that many of the new directors being appointed are joining a board for the first time.

There might be a three-year lead time to fill some board positions as directors retire or move on. But boards can't afford to passively wait. If the board has an urgent need for a particular expertise, it should go out and get it right away. And to make room for the new director, the committee should encourage an incumbent to retire sooner.

"We say board succession is an ongoing process and shouldn't be left to retirement or events," Roger Kenny says. Boards are increasingly coming to his firm, Boardroom Consultants, with forward-looking, ongoing board successions rather than just to execute an immediate search. An ongoing board succession process gives them time to contact potential directors now, get to know them, and let them get to know you. Don't assume a given director doesn't want to serve because he or she has rejected other offers. Board service is always more attractive when the prospective director knows the board has its act together—that the board is thorough in covering its bases and functions well as a group.

The governance committee must not only recruit new directors, but also design and execute a formal succession process that accommodates the *transition of directors off the board*. Research shows that boards are not perfect in selecting directors, nor are they courageous in moving out those directors who either were mistakenly selected or whose presence in the boardroom is hampering the board's effectiveness. My research has found a few companies that do informal reviews of each director, usually conducted by the CEO or governance committee chair. In those reviews it's not unusual to discover at least one director who is no longer welcome on the board. In any human group, some people progress while others regress. Given the speed of change, the process of transitioning directors off the board is a must for the board to remain a competitive advantage. A transition process also prevents excellent directors from leaving in frustration. I have personally known two situations in which very good directors resigned because of frustration with their colleagues.

Some companies put in term limits to avoid awkwardness and create a natural attrition of directors. Governance committees would do better to create a climate in which a director stepping down is not a sign of personal failure but rather one of *fit*. Individual directors, for their part, should be attuned to their own contributions and how they are affecting the board's dynamic. They shouldn't stay on a board for the wrong reasons (see sidebar).

In order to keep board composition in tune with the speed and architecture of external change, the governance committee should ask at least once per year: How do we figure out what our board needs? How do we get the right people for the job? What does the board succession process look like? How can the

Are You Staying on Your Board for the Right Reasons?

Just as a board succession process requires a board to add members as needed, it also implies that directors must leave. One of these days, you could be one of those directors and volunteer to move on. Don't forget, there is more demand for than supply of good directors. You will be needed on other boards.

Board transitions are often perceived skeptically in the press, who like to infer that the transition represents either discord on the board or a director's inability to contribute. This can make it awkward for boards to make changes to their memberships and for directors to step down. But having a formal board succession process and letting shareholders know about it actually makes it easier to leave a board without the departure being viewed negatively. The company's reputation will remain intact—and so will yours.

Some boards have mandatory retirement ages. While directors may grumble at the arbitrary ages at which they must step down, mandatory retirement offers the benefit of creating a natural transition for the board to inject itself with fresh blood. And whether or not a board has a mandatory retirement age, it should consider having a diversity of ages present at all times in order to allow for attrition over time.

What I've also found is that conscientious directors will want to stay on a board for as long as they think they are making a contribution. And when they feel their contribution is dropping, they start to put feelers out for other opportunities.

On the other hand, there are a few individuals who fight to stay on a board because of the prestige, regardless of their contribution. *It is the job of the governance committee to decide* when it's time for someone to move on—whether it's because they've served for fifteen years or because they're not adding enough to the boardroom dialogue. The committee should do it gracefully, of course, and not make it seem like it is pushing the individual out. "The Lead Director or the head of the governance committee needs to be able to tell directors, 'You've done a great job, but that chair needs to be filled by someone with x, y, z skills,'" says Roger Kenny, president of Boardroom Consultants. It's the committee's duty to keep the board fresh and effective with a relevant mix of expertise.

If you find yourself in the position where, reading in between the lines, you hear the governance committee suggesting that you not serve for another year, hear the committee out and have the maturity to recognize that your expertise may no longer be crucial to that company. Better yet, sense when a change is needed before such situations arise. Anticipating when it's time to leave gives you the chance to explore other opportunities to wield your expertise.

governance committee improve board succession? Clearly, the board of Citigroup, among others, failed at this role prior to the subprime mortgage meltdown.

Once a year, the governance committee should present its deliberations on board composition and succession to the board, as well as its future plans for making the board the best it can be. In doing that, it must address:

1. The anticipated requirements of the board composition over five to ten years. Staggering the ages of directors on a board is important—that's why a ten-year view is needed.

2. A clear plan of what will be required, in stages, of nominating new directors, including the process of recruiting those directors, the time line, the pipeline of candidates, and the interview priorities. If three directors are expected to retire in the next five years, for example, how will those slots get filled?

3. The skills currently present on the board that are not going to be required or should be reduced in concentration (to make room for new skills).

4. The process of de-nominating directors—including board members who have become ineffective. The board's self-evaluation and peer evaluation are vital inputs to this process.

This is a serious responsibility. It demands commitment, time, and meticulous attention. If the governance committee is not actively working on board succession, every director should feel empowered to raise the question.

However, I don't want to give the impression that the mix of directors alone determines the effectiveness of a board. Far from it, in fact. Some of the greatest governance failures in history, like Enron, have taken place with a world-class assemblage of directors on their boards. These were highly decorated individuals with (previously) impeccable resumes. Rather, it takes a lot of other factors, including group dynamics, effective leadership, and each individual's personal adoption of the ownership mindset, for the directors to combine into an effective board.

Key Points

- Hardworking, conscientious boards can fail when their members lack crucial expertise.

- Boards must do their own succession planning with lead time to ensure they have the right mix of skills, experience, and expertise at all times. The board as a whole must be able to add value and provide proper oversight on the range of issues that are emerging.

- Personality is a hugely important criterion in selecting directors. Directors must be able to work well together for the board to be effective and yet be independent.

Table 1.1 Sample Directors' Skills Matrix

	Senior Leadership Experience (CEO/President)	Business Development/M&A Expertise	Financial Expertise (CFO)[1]	Public Board Experience	Diversity	Independence	Innovation	Industry Expertise (Aerospace or wireless)	Operational/Manufacturing Expertise	Global Expertise (Especially China)	IT/Technical Expertise (Academic/Industry)	Brand Marketing Expertise	Government Expertise (State or Federal)	Governance/Legal Expertise
Ellsbury	X	X	X	X		X	X	X	X	X		X		
Pedroia	X			X		X	X							
Ortiz	X	X	X	X	X	X		X	X	X			X	
Ramirez			X	X	X	X			X		X	X		
Drew	X	X		X		X		X		X				
Lowell	X			X		X			X		X			X
Youkilis	X			X		X		X	X			X		
Varitek				X		X		X	X	X			X	
Lugo	X					X				X			X	
Matsuzaka	X	X				X	X	X		X		X		X

[1]As defined under Sarbanes-Oxley § 404

- The governance committee owns the process of having the right composition of the board at all times. The committee must have a clear process on what skills and experiences will be needed when, and how changes will be made along the way.

Table 1.1 is an illustrative example of a directors' skills matrix, adapted from one used by a successful board. The names and skills have been modified from the original for anonymity.

Question 2.

ARE WE ADDRESSING THE RISKS THAT COULD SEND OUR COMPANY OVER THE CLIFF?

It's the success or unintentional negligence of the board that lets companies like Bear Stearns fail under the same conditions in which JP Morgan survived. No board can ever be omniscient, but there's no excuse for the boards of companies like Lehman Brothers and Washington Mutual, who witnessed the explicit warning shots when Bear Stearns was forced to sell to JP Morgan but still couldn't save their companies. Their boards failed to address the risks that put their companies' existence in danger. Had the boards been more engaged with the risk management process, examining the information available to them and observing management's priorities, they could have saved the jobs and pensions of thousands of employees.

Deeply disappointed employees and other constituencies are pointing their fingers at the boards of those companies, taking them to task for the companies' failures. A trial lawyer in Washington mentioned in 2008 that he is certain that there will be a flood of shareholder suits—against directors, not just CEOs or executives. The signs are clear: in the future, boards had better put more emphasis on understanding total enterprise risk.

That puts a huge burden on boards—particularly given the rising complexity of risk. Risks come from internal sources (like the crooked culture and accounting irregularities at Enron or WorldCom, for example) or external sources (like the financial crisis of 2008 or the steep inflation in energy, transportation, and commodities prices in 2007). Slow-moving trends, like global climate change, can erupt into real risks overnight. Or some trends can move very fast as Detroit automakers found out in early 2008 when oil hit $140 a barrel and American consumers abruptly stopped buying their profitable fleets of SUVs.

Boards have no choice but to get better at anticipating risk, scanning widely to detect diverse sources of risk and imagining how they might combine. But they also have to make risk a more central part of the content of their reviews of operations and performance. They have to drill more deeply to link managerial decisions with the risks associated with them, looking not just at risk to the P&L but also to the balance sheet. Management may use formulas to estimate charge-offs that reflect certain types of risk, projecting such things as write-offs for bad debts or obsolete inventory. But the ability to refinance short-term debt and other liquidity issues must also be considered, especially in the context of the global financial system. Compensation, too, should be linked to the health of and risk to the balance sheet as well as items on the P&L.

Every board has to think of risk more broadly and more often, before full-blown crises develop. To do that, boards should use different lenses to detect potential vulnerabilities. And they need better preparedness, including clear risk management processes for the board and management, contingency plans, and a set of advisors on call.

How You Can Use Different Lenses to Examine Risk

Complexity and volatility in the business environment are greater than ever. They are causing more extreme and diverse sources of risk. Cross-industry disruptions are becoming more prevalent, and new players, including government entities, are flexing their muscles in some parts of the globe. More government regulation is likely to be in the offing. The complexity of the global financial system hides risk in unexpected places. And all these risks—the known and the unexpected—can combine in dangerous ways to create perfect storms, for example, plunging housing prices and lack of liquidity in financial markets. Missing on risk can wipe out a decade's worth of shareholder value.

Boards can better track the ever-expanding range of risks by defining the potential sources and viewing risk through each of those lenses. The most important lens for tracking risk is financial. Boards have to keep a close watch on vulnerabilities in the health and management of the balance sheet. But look, too, at strategy and operations, politics and geopolitics, reputation, and corporate culture, keeping in mind that the seemingly improbable so-called hundred-year flood might well occur during your board's tenure. These five lenses will help any board reduce the chances of an unpleasant surprise. Some boards may want to add other categories of risk to the five presented here. Other examples include information technology and intellectual property.

The Financial Vulnerability Lens

More boards need to be attuned to their companies' financial vulnerability, because events in the capital markets and the global financial system can turn against the company, the industry, or the economy very quickly. Early in 2008, the board of a $10 billion industrial company suggested to its CEO: "Conditions could worsen and we're not confident about continued access to short-term capital in the credit markets. Do whatever you need to do to conserve cash and maintain liquidity, even if securing financing now means paying a slightly higher interest rate."

That advice proved to be prescient seven months later, when credit markets froze up. Companies that used revolvers for financing found the taps had run dry, virtually overnight. Even companies with approved, legally binding credit lines became nervous that September, when some banks reneged on commitments. What had seemed a remote possibility at the start of the year was not far-fetched to this company's board. The company took a hit by paying a higher interest rate but ended up in stronger financial shape than any of its competitors.

The board should watch cash flows—everybody knows cash is king—as an early warning signal of distress. To do that, directors need to see very clearly where cash is coming from and where it is going. And by that I mean all of the cash, not just the sources that appear on the balance sheet. Then the board can stress-test liquidity under different assumptions to see how the company's cash flow could change. Don't take for granted that cash will be available from current sources when trouble arrives. The board has to know what happens to cash under extreme conditions and what the contingency plans are for it to understand how vulnerable the company is. An individual company's financial risk does not exist in isolation from the global financial system, so boards have to consider a range of impacts.

A related question is the prudent level of debt and mix of debt vehicles. Many CEOs and CFOs make a big deal about lowering the cost of debt by five basis points. There's nothing wrong with that, as long as the small print hidden in the debt covenants is well understood.

These elements of financial vulnerability should be at the top of directors' minds as conditions change. For example, one highly leveraged manufacturer was bidding on a major contract that required a lot of advance funding. The board got to know the contract well because it was part of both the spending and revenue sides of a budget discussion. In addition, the balance sheet summarized the firm's leverage and the debt covenants attached to its lending vehicles.

A few months later, the company got news that it didn't win the contract, despite its heavy investment. When the announcement was made, the chair of the audit committee immediately thought of the possible connection between the contract and the balance sheet. She called the CFO at home and asked whether the decision would affect the company's debt. "I'm glad you asked. It'll be tight, but we'll be fine," the CFO said. "There won't be a debt rating downgrade, and the rest of the business is generating cash, so there's no risk of violating any debt covenants." That director was acutely attuned to financial vulnerability—and, as a result, so was management.

A company can lose its freedom if its finances leave it vulnerable. The availability of cash and credit is as much a function of market confidence as of logic; if that confidence is broken, no logic will protect you. And when liquidity drops, shareholder value falls even faster. Short sellers come out like vultures and leave the company exposed to takeovers. Many companies have very quickly become acquisition targets after a stock price decline. Clark Equipment is one of them; in 1995 it was acquired by Ingersoll Rand in a hostile attack launched within a week of its stock price decline.

Unanticipated currency movements can also leave a company financially vulnerable. In 2008, Anheuser-Busch, the dominant beer market shareholder in the U.S., was acquired by Belgian-based InBev, a move that might have been inconceivable three years earlier before the dollar devalued by a quarter in two years. Exchange rates reversed before the transaction closed, but InBev still went through with it.

The Strategy and Operations Lens

Risk is an integral part of every company's strategy; when boards review strategy, they have to be forceful in asking the CEO what risks are inherent in the strategy. They need to explore "what ifs" with management in order to stress-test against external conditions such as recession or currency exchange movements. This will give the board a sense for the business risks the company faces— and allows them to probe whether the CEO is being realistic and whether the management team is prepared for contingencies.

Concentrations of customer bases are a particular strategic risk. Entire customer segments can disappear overnight, as makers of networking gear like Lucent and Nortel found out when they depended too much on dot-com companies. One construction services firm gets 80 percent of its revenues from two long-term contracts with retail chains. When one of the customers began to falter, it halted expansion and had trouble paying its bills. The board should have made sure management had anticipated that risk and found a way to expand the customer base. It should have also made sure management had a contingency plan for meeting its short-term revolving debt service if the customer disappeared.

Risk pops up in operational reviews, as well. Monitoring is not just about making the numbers, but also about talking through the risks. Take one low-margin apparel manufacturer, which for fifteen years had not raised its prices, selling through major department stores. In 2007, cotton prices were going through the roof. In its operational review, the board needed to know whether management could pass price increases on to the customer. With high leverage, the company's lack of pricing power would shrink margins and squeeze the highly leveraged company for cash. That's a big risk. Combine that possibility with expectations of a weakening retail sector and the board gets a clear picture that the apparel maker's financial health could be in real trouble.

Managing risk does not entail eliminating it; the competence required is how to assess it and how to manage it. If you have no appetite for risk, you shouldn't be on a board; it will inhibit the CEO from making bold and necessary moves and potentially company-saving strategic bets.

On the other hand, boards also need to watch the CEO's appetite for risk: some are almost gamblers (directors would say, "he can be reckless") and some are too risk averse. Some CEOs are serial gamblers who can't help making splashy strategic bets—some of which do turn out to be winners. Other CEOs delude themselves into thinking they are conservative, not realizing that by not taking risks, they may be subjecting the company to the biggest risk of all. Think back to the 1970s when having a clean balance sheet and strong assets made a company prey to corporate raiders. Or to the failure of cash-rich companies like AOL and Microsoft to invest what they needed to build a world-class search engine, either because they did not see Google coming or they were not able to take the risk. It's up to the board to make sure the company and its CEO have the appropriate appetite for strategic risk.

The Political and Geopolitical Lens

Geopolitical risks can become real very suddenly, wiping out whole industries, and boards need to stay on top of them. New regulation can change the dynamics of entire industries. In 2006 and 2007, foreign governments were increasingly flexing their muscles and using natural resources as a source of leverage. If they reduce significantly the supply of a raw material or raise the price of their material by an order of magnitude, it can bring a company to its knees. So the board needs to explore what dependencies the company has and how it can manage them both for its own survival and for competitive advantage.

For example, BP took a huge risk when it began investing in Russia in the 1990s, and for many years it was considered ahead of the game in a key emerging source of fossil fuels. Since forming its TNK-BP joint venture in 2003, however, political conditions have changed. Those are risky types of bets that boards have to vet at the time of the decision and monitor continuously.

Boards should utilize the political and geopolitical lens in two key ways. First, they have to gain access to important figures—diplomats, politicians, policymakers, think-tank fellows, or anyone else with a deep knowledge and current understanding of the public sector and geopolitical affairs. Boards can invite

experts to speak with them over dinner, or make sure to participate in gatherings where they are able to interact. Having someone such as Tony Blair, for example, share personal insights on
the next round of European Union enlargement could be invalu-
able for a board doing business in Eastern Europe and Russia.
They could keep the board abreast of crucial developments and
help think through the implications for the company and the
industry.

Boards can also assemble advisory boards of such individuals to formalize the relationships. They might consider this
when they need more frequent access to the experts' insights,
for example, regarding regulatory development and enforcement
in Washington. And they might ask advisory board members
to facilitate contact with policymakers. At least one company
has had former SEC officials speak privately with lawmakers to
make sure regulators were fully informed and didn't blindside
companies based on partial understanding of the issues.

The Reputation Lens

In this age of transparency, an idea or rumor can spread instantly
across the Internet like a virus. The court of public opinion is
as crucial as ever, as stakeholders ranging from customers and
investors to NGOs and policymakers increasingly speak their
minds. And their voices are being heard: a bad reputation can
pressure a company's stock price, its business prospects, and its
ability to recruit top talent.

Hits to a company's reputation can stem from any number
of sources, ranging from disgruntled employees and customers to investors, communities, and regulators. Just the threat of
litigation or a Wells notice from the Securities and Exchange
Commission can have a big impact on a company's reputation.
And anonymous websites that criticize the company's customer
service probably indicate a declining reputation and a potential
crisis. Wal-Mart is one of many companies that have been taken
to task anonymously online.

Directors can be very valuable sounding boards for CEOs; they can help management assess whether a setback is temporary or whether it is the tip of an iceberg that needs to be addressed. And they can help determine whether the criticism has any substance. Some companies have been blind to the factors that caused their reputations to fade, even though they had plenty of time do something about it. Sometimes the CEO disagrees so strongly with the critics that he or she just can't see the merit of the argument, or he resents outsiders challenging practice he believes to be in the company's best interest. The board can step in and advise the CEO when action as well as communication is needed. The Wal-Mart board prodded CEO Lee Scott to pay more attention to stakeholders' complaints, including its workers' wages and health care provision and its environmental footprint. It took an enormous commitment of Scott's time, and he found it very exhausting, but Scott's response improved the firm's reputation and staved off a crisis, even if some of the company's critics never go away.

The People and Culture Lens

The board can't know everything that is happening inside the company, but it has to have ways to sense whether the company's culture or some of its leaders are putting the company at risk. Boards have to have an ear to the ground to pick up clues that things aren't quite right in the organization, and directors have to be willing to put their soft impressions and hunches on the table and seek ways to confirm or refute them. And of course the board should waste no time taking action when problems are evident.

The CEO is the face of the company and boards must hold their chief executives to a high ethical standard. Sometimes circumstances warrant fast action. Time Warner moved quickly to remove Home Box Office CEO Chris Albrecht after he was arrested for assaulting a girlfriend in Las Vegas. Boeing's board moved quickly to ask CEO Harry Stonecipher to resign after an investigation determined that he was having a relationship with an executive, against the company's code of conduct. Breaches of ethics are unacceptable from the leaders who are supposed to set the tone for the rest of the organization.

Boards must also watch for a toxic culture that enables ethical lapses throughout the organization. Companies set rules—but the culture determines how employees follow them. It's a board's job to know the company's culture well enough to know whether its practices are sound and its reputation is not at risk. Incentives should not promote risky behavior—including bribery or other shady practices in developing countries. A rogue employee is one thing, but many companies have found systemic approaches to circumventing rules behind the scenes. Siemens has had to deal with investigations by three European nations about alleged bribery from secret bank accounts to secure business overseas. At best, management and the board either didn't care or didn't want to know.

Boards should insist on getting regularly briefed on company training to prevent corruption and bribery, as well as how health and safety standards are being met in the company's plants and those of its supply chain partners. Asking the questions sets the tone that poor practices will not be tolerated.

Boards can also learn about the culture without needing to hear it from the CEO and his or her team. One way is to have directors go into the organization to get some feel for the culture of line managers and workers in plants, stores, and offices. Another is to conduct periodic "pulse surveys," as General Electric calls them, which ask a sample of employees fifteen to twenty questions in an online survey just to put a finger on the pulse of the company.

How a Risk Committee Helps the Company's Preparedness

Risk management is a big job for boards. Many boards realize they need to own enterprise risk, but a consensus has not emerged on how to manage it at the board level. As they emerge from the financial crisis of 2008, they know they can't wait any longer to address it by delegating responsibilities within the board, by ensuring management has accountability and processes to work with the board on risk management, and by ensuring the board and management have taken every appropriate preparedness measure.

I recommend that a board form a stand-alone risk committee, which would work with the audit committee. In the 1990s, the Citigroup board had a committee that looked primarily at country risk, from the political and currency exchange perspectives. Had that committee expanded its scope to include more types of risk, it might have done a better job getting ahead of subprime mortgages. General Electric, on the other hand, has a public responsibility committee that has broadened its scope over the years to include a range of risks.

Other boards take a holistic view of the risks faced, divide the risks into meaningful groups, and assign them to committees. The audit committee has a big enough role as it is, so non-audit-related risk management should be assigned elsewhere. The governance committee might take a prominent role, but if so, the committee's charter should explicitly define the committee's risk management responsibility.

Regardless of committee structure, the idea is to ensure the board sets aside the time to talk about risk explicitly. Risk has to go on the twelve-month priorities and it has to be part of the agenda of a board meeting, at least once per year, with management discussing how the sources of risk are evolving. The risk committee itself should meet formally at least twice per year.

The board also needs to make sure management has a methodology to explore and manage risk. Management has to assign someone to be accountable for working with the board on risk and for defining processes to manage enterprise risk. If the company is climbing out of hot water, the board might even suggest that the CEO hire a chief risk officer. Or management might form its own internal risk team, consisting of the general counsel and heads of public relations, finance, and investor relations. The internal risk team would be responsible for making sure practices regarding the environment, health and safety, anti-discrimination, bribery, and all other processes comply with local and international standards. It would also prepare action plans for crises.

If conditions warrant, the board's risk committee can commission the internal risk team to audit a process to make sure business practices are up to snuff, say, on the health and safety of workers. In those cases, it should define what needs to be audited, by whom, and how often. The risk committee should also keep open lines of communication throughout the company to ensure that problems at any level will come to its attention. If the board does not listen to potential whistleblowers and take their reports very seriously, the whistleblowers' next phone call could be to regulators, law enforcement, or the press, and a crisis will ensue.

Part of risk management is also preparedness, so the risk committee should work with management to ensure there are action plans in the event of a crisis. The risk committee should take charge of keeping experts on call, coordinating the effort with management. Former government officials, for example, can provide insights and coordinate responses to regulators. Investment banks can quickly analyze hostile bids if they arise. If a major lawsuit hits the company's reputation, attorneys will be needed. And public relations and media experts will be needed for virtually any type of crisis. All those advisors need to be lined up in advance of the worst-case scenario coming to pass.

Key Points

- Boards have to think broadly about risk and dig deep to understand its many sources. Consider how risks might combine in a perfect storm, and link managerial decisions with risk to the balance sheet as well as the P&L.

- Boards can get a better handle on risk by viewing the business and the landscape through different lenses. Financial risk is one of several important lenses.

- Financial risk must be viewed in the context of the global financial system.

- Consider creating a risk committee to dig deeper into potential sources of risk. But the full board should discuss risk explicitly at least once a year.

Question 3.

ARE WE PREPARED TO DO OUR JOB WELL WHEN A CRISIS ERUPTS?

Crises can strike any corporation without notice, potentially destroying huge amounts of shareholder value. When crises occur, they divert the attention of both management and the board, sapping precious human energy. Many companies are right now in the midst of a crisis caused by the meltdown of the global financial system. Their leaders can hardly focus on anything other than trying to anticipate when the next bomb will drop and how to deal with the fallout.

The lesson is that boards have to do their level best to prevent crises, but they can't prevent them all. So they must also be prepared to take charge and do damage control when a crisis erupts, even if it is something they have never experienced before.

There are basically two types of crises: those that are knowable, meaning they happen from time to time but at unpredictable intervals and with varying ferocity, and those that are unknowable, meaning no one has even imagined such an event. Boards have to prepare for both the knowable unknowns and the unknowable ones in order to minimize disruption to the business, damage to the brand and company reputation, and loss of hard cash.

The Knowable Unknowns

I believe that any kind of crisis that has previously taken place anywhere in the world belongs in the category of *knowable unknowns*. They should not be a complete surprise, and some expertise will exist somewhere to deal with them. Boards need to benchmark these practices as a preparedness measure.

Some crises are internally inflicted, including some situations created by management: loading the balance sheet with high debt that can cripple the company if external conditions deteriorate; relying heavily on very few customers; failing to enforce compliance on safety, health, and environmental regulations; engaging in unethical practices such as price fixing; and providing lax oversight of operations, which delays a major launch (the Airbus-380 and Boeing-787 faced several consecutive long delays, for example).

Boards can cause a crisis, too, for instance, by leaking information to the press or taking their board business public. In 2002, a frustrated member of the HP board led a proxy battle to block the company's planned merger with Compaq. The distrust lingered long after the event, and the board subsequently decided not to renominate him. Management and the board couldn't help but be distracted by the daily media scrutiny.

Boards also can create a crisis when they have a tin ear to shareholder complaints for too long. "You cannot be an ostrich when it comes to investors," Nell Minow, editor and co-founder of The Corporate Library, was quoted as saying. Ignoring mounting criticism doesn't make it go away. Expressing confidence in a CEO publicly and then letting him or her go days later seriously damages the board's credibility. Only a few days before Citigroup CEO Chuck Prince saw the writing on the wall and resigned, the board made statements of strong support for him. It even got Prince Al Waleed, a major investor since the early 1990s, to declare his full support.

Crises from outside the company are increasingly common. Wal-Mart got caught by surprise by public coalitions who protested employee wages and benefits and got the attention of the media. The issue picked up ferocious speed and momentum and terrified management (not to mention stockholders) as it began to damage the company's brand and reputation. Top management was shocked and failed to deal with it for a long period of time.

Product recalls can be triggered by external sources. The case in which Tylenol was contaminated produced a lot of lessons for anyone who has to deal with such a crisis. Coca-Cola experienced similar crises in Belgium and India, where Pepsi also had the safety of its product called into question. Both companies handled their crises less decisively than Johnson & Johnson did.

A more unusual type of crisis has emerged in the area of mergers and acquisitions when companies come under a protracted attack. Microsoft's attack on Yahoo! is a recent example. Microsoft has been coming in and out of the fray and letting tension drag on in a very fast technology game beset by flattening or even declining revenue. This behavior is distracting the Yahoo! board and management to no end, and the market value of Yahoo! has taken a pounding.

Boards should first of all watch for these crises while they are in the making. The problem might lie in shareholder communications that are vague about the company's strategic direction or other areas that can be easily remedied. Poor relations with regulators, for example, can incite criticism and later erupt into a full-blown crisis, but the problem may be fixable by coaching the CEO or encouraging her to bring in additional talent. It makes sense for the board to have a lengthy discussion in executive session about the substance of any criticism they are picking up on and to explore the possibility of corrective action.

Headlines are rife with stories of crises that could have been detected and dealt with. Take, for instance, the case of a CEO who charms the board and the external public but is toxic to everyone inside. Subordinates steadily depart and yes men, who tolerate the abuse because they are compensated handsomely, take their place. Such a problem can erupt into a crisis if the dysfunctional behavior crosses legal bounds, for instance, or the displaced leaders begin to go public. In one such case, the general counsel mustered the courage to speak to the board, which used a third party to administer a 360 evaluation on the CEO. Directors were horrified to discover what was happening and immediately removed the CEO, appointing a director as the interim leader.

Every board needs to decide which categories are important enough to prepare for ahead of time. The role for boards is to ensure that management has considered them and has appropriate mechanisms and processes in place to deal with a range of threats. Some companies have a core group that forms a crisis committee comprising the CEO, general counsel, CFO, and a public relations and communications officer. Additional members can be called on depending on the nature of the problem. The plans should be updated as new information becomes available. In each case, there must be a point person in charge and a game plan that can be deployed instantly. One of the key ingredients of the game plan is the ability to communicate extensively on short notice to get and send information to the right people. Former Coca-Cola CEO Doug Ivester waited one week before making a public statement after dozens of Belgian youth fell ill drinking Coke in June 1999, despite at least one board member counseling him to speak immediately. It took months to restore Coca-Cola's reputation in Europe.

The plans should be reviewed by the appropriate committee of the board, perhaps the risk committee. The committee should decide who the point person will be for the board and establish its own procedures for contacting all directors. An audit committee member might be a good choice for financial crises, for example, while a director with a legal or public policy background could play the role in some other circumstances. It should lay the ground rules for ensuring decisions are not delayed because board approval is needed.

The committee and the point director must be psychologically equipped to have a steady hand to calm the nerves of the various players, including perhaps a CEO who is getting rattled, when a crisis arrives. Preparing a list of advisors or experts available to the board 24/7 and keeping contact information current can save valuable time in the heat of the moment. Periodically rehearsing a crisis can test how well the mechanisms and processes are working.

How to Deal with Unknowable Unknowns

The *unknowable unknowns* are impossible to detect before they erupt, even though they might be brewing for some time, because no one has ever seen them before. When they do become apparent, the impact is hard to predict. No one knows how long or deep the problem might be. Boards and management must prepare for them nonetheless by using their usual crisis plan with two major differences. First, the people and teams assigned to confront such a crisis need to have the skills to seek and sift through information from a large variety of sources and construct multiple scenarios on the fly. They must have the confidence to act decisively and construct worst case scenarios even when many factors are unknown and ambiguous. And second, the board must be prepared to take the lead.

During the crisis, the point person from the board must stay in close touch with management as they sort out what is happening. Here the board can be an important check on management's interpretation of events, because even the best CEOs can sometimes be too optimistic or have blind spots. Rich Noll, CEO of Hanesbrands, comments: "The board makes sure that we're not just working on one plan, but rather on a broad range of scenarios. They help us think about the unknowable; make sure we're managing the 'black swan' type of risks, in addition to the things you can predict." At the same time, directors can share their own experiences from analogous situations to help fill in management's blind spots. "People tend to be too optimistic or too pessimistic," says Noll. "The board can help management maintain a balanced perspective."

The board should also help management imagine what the domino effect might be, projecting what other problems might arise as one thing triggers something else. Take, for instance, a company that is facing imminent liquidity problems. If the lenders sense the company's problems, a vicious cycle can begin in which the cost of borrowing increases, credit tightens further, and terms of refinancing become onerous, all exacerbating pressure on management and the management of cash. At the first sign of a cash crisis, boards have to keep asking where cash is coming from and going to as they weigh different scenarios and courses of action. This deliberation includes all sources of cash commitments, whether on or off the balance sheet. Which partnerships or leases is the company locked into, and which customers or suppliers are at risk? If something starts to shift in the wrong direction, what else might happen? Those considerations will help management formulate a realistic Plan B or C.

The board must be prepared to take charge if management is slow to grasp the situation and take the lead. Consider the unprecedented financial meltdown in 2008, which left no one untouched on a worldwide basis and left many people without the nest egg they had spent decades building. Why was it an unknowable unknown? The global financial system spun out of its regular rhythm and went out of control. It never occurred to anyone that such a thing could happen. Corporations have faced high leverage and tight credit before, but not the breakdown of the whole financial system and such an abrupt constriction of money flows. It made some business models inoperative, and boards had to engage immediately to try to take their companies to safety.

Waiting for management to make a move is a mistake. Management, after all, has never been tested under the conditions of an unknowable unknown, and the board cannot assume that they know how to respond. Obviously, the boards of Lehman Brothers, Bear Stearns, General Motors, and many others failed to realize that their management was not able to sense the magnitude and cope with this tsunami.

Some boards took charge of the dire situation and moved fast. In some cases they fired the CEO (as at Merrill Lynch); in other cases they reaffirmed their confidence in the CEO and the management team. Their communication became very frequent as they worked hard to stay synchronized and ahead of the changing picture. In one company, the board met six times in two months, and yes, all directors attended all those meetings and were instantly available to make rapid decisions. Any delay or less engagement on the part of the board could have been disastrous for the shareholders and employees of that company.

Key Points

- Boards have to be vigilant to prevent crises and ensure that management is well prepared for the *knowable unknowns*.
- When an *unknowable unknown* strikes, the challenge is to sort through the ambiguity fast and imagine different scenarios and ramifications.
- Boards may have to take the lead when an emergency situation arises to keep people informed, steady people's nerves, and help management sort through the ambiguity.

Question 4.

ARE WE WELL PREPARED TO NAME OUR NEXT CEO?

Every director knows deep down that nothing is more important than having the right CEO at all times. Yet it's clear that many boards are not fully owning up to this responsibility. They wait too long to make a change (sometimes beyond the point of no return), and they don't get to know the organization's up-and-coming leaders well enough or soon enough.

Boards need to go on the offensive and take charge of who leads the company, the way a few boards have begun to do. In the past eighteen months, two boards replaced CEOs who had achieved record earnings over their tenures of five years or more. Both CEOs were considered very successful, and there were absolutely no issues of ethics or personality. It was simply time, those boards decided, for the company to switch gears. Although these boards placed high value on their CEOs' previous contributions, they became convinced that a leader with a different set of skills would be better suited for the new times.

In one of the companies, among the global leaders in its industry, the board came to the conclusion in executive session that it had the opportunity of a lifetime, given capital market conditions, to make mega-scale acquisitions and grow dramatically larger. The incumbent CEO disagreed with the strategy, preferring to rely on the organic growth that had saved the company from bankruptcy and driven his success over the past three years. So the board went outside and recruited a well-respected CEO who had a track record of both organic growth and M&A. It's too soon to know the outcome of that decision, but the point is that the board made a judgment about what the company needed at that time and took the initiative to put the appropriate leader at the helm.

Not many boards have owned up to that extent. Individual directors care quite a bit about succession, but most boards need to raise their game to ensure the company has the right leadership at all times. Boards should have clear, well thought out processes for dealing with succession and devote more time and energy to it. They should be prepared for the following:

1. *Making a selection within the next two to three years.* Do you really have a list of strong internal candidates from which to choose a CEO when the incumbent is scheduled to retire? Is that pool diverse enough to produce candidates who fit different conditions that might arise? Has the board moved quickly to test candidates and suggest ways to fill gaps in their leadership capabilities?

2. *Spotting high-potential leaders early on.* Do you have a process for identifying young high-potential leaders, following and perhaps accelerating their development through different experiences and engaging with them at different stages of their careers?

3. *Facing the worst case.* Has the full board discussed who would become CEO in the case of an emergency? Do you review that name every year, and as conditions change?

Unless the answer to each question is an emphatic "yes," you have work to do. The management development and compensation committee or its equivalent should take the lead in this area and devote whatever time and energy is required. But ensuring strong leadership and smooth transitions is the board's primary responsibility, and thus every director must work hard to get it right.

Selecting the CEO

"I get an F for succession planning," Sandy Weill told *Fortune* magazine, referring to the process that led to Chuck Prince taking the reins of Citigroup from Weill. Weill is a stand-up guy for being accountable, but he's wrong: the whole board of Citigroup gets an F.

The succession process culminates with the selection of a CEO, and let's be absolutely clear: the board, not the outgoing CEO, selects the CEO. Yes, the CEO's input is valuable, but there should be no question that in today's corporate governance environment, the board owns that decision.

Ideally, the CEO selection process would begin two to three years in advance of a planned succession. That gives the board enough time to conduct a rigorous assessment of the business and its external context and from that to define the job's nonnegotiable criteria. It also allows time to get to know leaders in depth and create fuller, more accurate depictions of each candidate so the board can make a sound judgment about who is best suited for the job.

Start with the Strategy and Its Context

When boards start talking about CEO succession, they tend to start talking about people first. Most companies have a short list of people considered to be contenders for the top job. But the succession process should start in earnest with a dispassionate view of the company's strategic direction and the business environment. This is the time to be sure the board is looking forward in understanding—I mean *really* understanding—what is happening with the company and industry in the context of the broad macro environment. What issues in the macro environment might be relevant? And what specific challenges is the company facing now, and what is it likely to face in the next few years? Does the company have to grow fast, consolidate, expand into a new industry, or radically change its course? Directors should be continuously picking up clues about these things by absorbing external information, visiting sites, and asking the CEO for updates on markets and competition. Some boards even invite experts on external changes to speak to them as a group in order to get a variety of views. That knowledge will point to the qualities and skills the next CEO will need.

The whole board also has to be on the same page regarding the company's strategy. If they haven't had in-depth discussions and reached consensus on where the company is headed or what it needs, they have to do so before they begin to talk about CEO candidates. The CEO job may be very different from what it has been in the past. The board of one health care company, for example, recognized that the industry would be in flux because of the unresolved policy debate in Washington. Directors had become familiar with the debate and were convinced that a consumer-oriented revolution in health care was on its way. They came to a consensus that the ability to help shape the future of health care policy would be vital to the company's future. That became an essential, non-negotiable criterion for the board when it compared two highly qualified candidates for succession. The board passed over a highly talented leader known for his great operational skills in favor of a second candidate who had never run such a large organization but was a broad thinker, highly adept at leading external constituencies and managing relationships, and well-attuned to the consumer experience. The board followed up by making sure the new CEO got support to shore up her operating capabilities. That CEO selection has been proving to be a good one.

Narrow the Field

With an understanding of where the company is headed and what it is likely to need in its future leader, the board can focus on a short list of candidates created in conjunction with the

CEO and perhaps the head of human resources. Then the board can create opportunities to get to know the candidates really well, both personally and professionally, by inviting them to dinner, for instance, and having them present to the board. Some directors make a point of visiting future candidates on their turf and meeting their teams.

Some of the candidates may have gaps in their skills, or the board might have questions about their ability to handle certain situations. Directors can suggest that the CEO move the person into a job that expands her capabilities and tests her.

Even as the board looks for talented leaders one, two, and even three levels below the CEO, the reality is that many companies, even those that invest heavily in leadership development, need to consider an outsider for their next leader. If internal candidates don't appear to be meeting the criteria or are all cut from the same cloth, there may be no choice but to widen the field by going outside. Don't wait until the last minute. If there are a few years before the planned succession, outsiders can be brought in one or two levels below the CEO. The CEO has to be involved, and the organization might have to make some changes to accommodate the new executive. Unblocking jobs, even when it means removing people who are doing their job well but are not CEO candidates, is part of the succession process.

One board assessed its high-potentials and decided it did not have the bench strength to provide an internal successor several years down the road. The CEO, who has a good relationship with the board, agreed. So the company found two very highly regarded individuals from outside the company and appointed them to jobs two levels below the CEO. The company had to restructure a division to make room for one leader, and remove an executive who had been effective but had run out of runway to make room for the other. Now the CEO and the board are closely watching, hopeful that at least one of the two new executives develops into future CEO material.

Executive search firms are very good at finding external candidates, but the board has to be sure the search firm has a solid grounding in the business issues and the criteria. Some companies have expanded their field of CEO candidates by acquiring companies run by top-notch leaders. Vikram Pandit ended up as CEO of Citigroup less than a year after his investment firm, Old Lane Partners, was acquired by the financial services giant.

There are, of course, risks associated with bringing in an outsider at a high level. If the person fails in the job, company performance could take a hit, doubts could arise about whether the company can make a smooth leadership transition, and the search for a likely replacement has to start all over again. Still, it's always a good idea to test leaders internally and bring in outsiders sooner rather than later, preferably into positions that don't bet the ranch and without promises to promote the person to the top job on a certain timetable.

Set the Criteria

When the succession decision is about a year away, the board should take another hard look at the external environment and the business challenges and translate them into specific criteria for the CEO job. Generalities such as "intelligent," "visionary," "strategic thinker," or "great with people" will not be very helpful. The board has to keep digging until it can define the three, four, or five things that are crucial to succeed in that company at that time. These must-have characteristics are then "non-negotiable": without them, a candidate cannot even be considered.

In today's complex environment, deep expertise in an industry or domain is increasingly important. Every board must decide whether that importance meets the non-negotiable threshold. In financial services, for example, domain knowledge appears to be non-negotiable. But in 1993, the board of IBM did shareholders a tremendous service by discounting domain knowledge in favor of other criteria they deemed more important. Instead of choosing a technology wizard as CEO, the IBM board chose Lou Gerstner, who was running RJR Nabisco at the time. They chose him largely because of his business savvy, which is precisely what the company needed. The board's insight about the most pressing business issues led to a decision that surprised many people and saved the company.

Clarity around the non-negotiables is crucial, but other criteria will also come into play. Some boards find it useful to create separate categories for them, such as non-negotiables, personality and cognitive traits, and givens (which might include things like integrity, character, communication skills, and a motor for personal growth).

Make the Match

The board's most critical task is to find the best fit between the job's criteria and the candidate in the context of the present and the future. With the non-negotiable criteria in sharp focus, the board has to create a dispassionate assessment of what each candidate has to offer. The best, most accurate profiles emerge when boards take the time to step back and discuss each candidate in depth. Going into the succession process, there is usually a lead horse. Sometimes, it's the individual the CEO is pushing; other times, it is a high-profile external candidate investors prefer. And directors sometimes have their personal favorites. The board has to throw those preconceived ideas to the wind and open their minds to the possibility that a dark horse may ultimately prove to be the best option. As executive recruiter Dennis Carey of Korn/Ferry says, "In most cases, the CEO will have a preferred candidate and get him or her in front of the board more frequently than other candidates. The board gets comfortable with someone who's always there, coming into the board room, going to social events, interacting with directors. It's very positive. But it handicaps other legitimate candidates."

The best succession processes focus on each individual's strengths, or god-given talents. What is this individual really good at, and under what circumstances does this person thrive? As directors pool their perceptions and probe each other for evidence to back their opinions, vague impressions and personal biases quickly disappear and the group begins to find exactly what makes each leader tick. They are often surprised by what they discover about the person. Sometimes the discussion brings new information to light and latent talents get recognized. Other times, directors' outdated views are shaken loose when there's no real evidence to back them up.

Boards can round out their picture of the candidates by conducting 360 checks on internal candidates and doing rigorous reference-checking on external candidates. Some candidates have the charisma to impress a board, but the individual's peers and direct reports see a different picture. Careful reference checking through directors' contacts and social circles can also reveal a great deal, especially when the questions are specific and the relationships are close and informal.

One company conducted a "360 review" of its three internal candidates by talking to the individuals who work closest with the candidates, above, below, and at the same level in the organization. Boards can do this themselves, presuming either the committee chair, the non-executive chair, or the Lead Director has the time and feels confident he or she can remain objective about the individuals. In fact, it makes sense to have more than one person do the process jointly to reduce the subjectivity of the interviews. Otherwise, a search firm can be very useful.

In one such case, the board engaged Carey to interview about a dozen people in the organization who knew the three internal candidates well. Initial interviews were three or four hours long, plus follow-up phone calls. Carey took steps to stress the confidentiality of the interviews and conducted them offsite. Spending half a day with each interviewee and following up as needed, he gathered a ton of detail on the candidates' skill sets.

What do they bring to the table? Will they admit where they are deficient? Can they fill in their personal gaps? What worked for them in the past? Will it work for them in the future in the CEO job, which is a quantum change from what they have experienced before?

The nuances in those responses are as revealing as the statements themselves. The interviewer can make subtle inferences and then cross-check them against what other interviewees say. A really perceptive and skilled interviewer will pick up on cues and be able to account for internal politics and biases. For example, one VP made some strong statements about a candidate's impulsiveness. When Carey asked the VP to explain, he elaborated by saying, "We were in a meeting and without prompting [the candidate] said, 'We've got to sell the consumer business.'" Guess which division the VP worked in? Carey probed further, "Why do you think that was an impulsive statement? *Should* the company sell the consumer side of the business?" The VP didn't have very good answers and backed away from his initial assertions.

Carey's subsequent report provided a rich vein of objective data for the board to use in its decision. That company's non-executive chair also did some checking on his own, asking others in the organization similar questions. The conclusions matched Carey's findings, giving the board great confidence.

Even if they use a search firm, boards must hold the succession reins. Carey took care not to suggest one candidate over the others, but rather to compare and contrast them. He understood that the decision was ultimately the board's. "If a headhunter says, 'I placed so-and-so in the top job,'" Carey said, "it means the board failed." The whole board must take ownership not only of the process, but also of the content and output.

The company Carey advised ultimately decided that the CEO's original choice, the president of the company, wasn't as strong a selection as a different candidate. The board chose a different person, who they learned was more widely respected by peers and direct reports internally and who would bring higher energy to the job. The decision appears to be paying off, although, as in almost all other cases, the other candidates on the short list chose to leave the company. Few incentives offered by the board and the incoming CEO can change that sad truth. But 360 reviews can also build support internally for the successor. Inclusion in the decision-making process is a very powerful way to get buy-in from key employees.

No matter how strictly they adhere to the process, boards can never be assured that their choice of a CEO is correct. But their judgments do improve when they insist on getting the facts on the table and cross-check each other. The test is not only whether the board can make the right decision, but also how quickly it can admit that it did not.

Even when the new CEO is succeeding, succession can never be on the back burner. CEO tenures are getting shorter and shorter. Given how rapidly business cycles are changing, even in an ideal scenario, a CEO might stay in her position for only about ten years. A twenty-year term will be increasingly unusual, because the CEO will be likely to run out of capacity. Long tenures also block the promotion of new blood up and down the organization. Given how long it takes to develop leaders, succession has to be one of the issues that is always on the board's mind.

Spotting High-Potential Leaders Early

Knowing the company and its leadership pipeline really well over an extended time is the best preparation a board can have for making a monumentally important succession decision. Of course, boards can't know every leader in a big company, and they don't have to. But they should be familiar with more leaders than most are currently exposed to, and they should ensure that management not only has robust processes for leadership development, but also has taken an honest look at its bench strength. One of the greatest advantages of knowing the up-and-coming leaders is advance warning when the field falls short. That allows the board to convince the CEO to bring in outsiders or move people around when there's still sufficient time to test them.

It begins with knowing what the company has, in terms of both people and processes. Boards should periodically hear straight from the head of HR about the processes in place for leadership development, about the metrics that reveal how recruitment, development, and retention are progressing, and who the real up-and-comers are. It might be useful to benchmark those results against competitors in the talent market and how needs are changing. And if there are any deficiencies, the CEO should clarify what the top team is doing about it.

Directors shouldn't stop with hearing about leaders secondhand. Until recently, boards have come to know personally only the individuals who either attend board meetings regularly or occasionally present to the board. This exposure is very positive; backed up by performance metrics and the CEO's reports, directors can formally and informally make judgments about the quality of the bench at the highest levels. Every director should make a point to personally get to know over a period of several years the top ten to fifteen leaders several levels below the CEO. As they engage with the leaders at dinner, listen and question them during presentations, and visit them on-site, directors can form their opinions and back up the CEO's judgment about who are the most promising up-and-comers and how best to develop them.

Another set of future leaders is equally important, but only a few boards are reaching out to them. Some boards ask the CEO to occasionally talk about high-potentials further down in the organization, but very few spend real time on it. That has to become more formal: boards should make a point to get briefed by the CEO on the top fifty or so leaders, at least annually. And more of those leaders need to get personal exposure to directors, either in the boardroom, informally, or on-site. The Tyco Electronics board, for example, reviews a business unit in depth before each board meeting; part of that review involves personally meeting the leaders in that unit, and intensely reviewing the business unit's talent needs and the progress of development efforts.

That level of attention will lead to producing a stronger pool of potential future CEOs, a decade in advance. One $20 billion consumer-goods company with a reputation for great leadership development hired a leader in his mid-thirties from a competitor, quickly identified his potential, and moved him to a strategy position working with the CEO. For several years, the board saw how thoughtful and analytical the leader was and wanted to develop him further; future CEO was definitely a possibility. So the CEO promoted him to head of global advertising, where he'll get to know every business in every territory in the context of both customers and the competition. It's a big promotion and one that will demonstrate whether he can master the front-end of the business. The CEO and the board will be watching to see if his bandwidth and his knowledge of the company broaden sufficiently, and they are prepared to help him along the way.

Some board members are superb at spotting nascent leadership talent. Directors can change a young leader's career trajectory with simple comments such as: "I was impressed with Lauren's grasp of the Asian market. She can size things up fast and sees the broader context. Is she considered a high-potential?" Suddenly others begin to see Lauren in a new light. When these directors interact with high-potentials four or five times and watch how they present and answer questions, they get powerful reference points to create hypotheses or spot fatal flaws. Boards get a definite sense of high-potentials' analytical skills, the way they approach problems, and the results they produce. Then boards can challenge management to think more boldly and creatively about how to bring young leaders along faster, for example, by making a leap into a job several levels higher.

However, the board doesn't know everything about the individuals, because it doesn't see them in action or hear how they interact with their own direct reports. And as good as any given director's radar for people evaluation, he or she is just one person. As opinions begin to form, directors should be careful to cross-check their impressions in executive session with their peers and with the CEO. At one industrial company, a director was skeptical about a unit manager after a weak presentation to the board. The CEO urged her to keep an open mind and visit the manager on-site before rendering judgment about the leader's potential. After the visit, the director changed her mind. "I was wrong about [Steve]," she later admitted in executive session. "I didn't realize the bandwidth that was needed to run that business and he clearly has it. And I'm really impressed with the team he's built. It says something about his ability to motivate top talent." Other board members concurred with that revised assessment.

While boards have to get more involved with the company's leadership development, they also have to be careful to not overstep their role. Some CEOs routinely inform their boards when they're changing the people in the top two layers, which is a good practice. But boards have to know how to interpret that information. A constant reshuffling or replacement of defectors could be a sign of deeper trouble.

The choice of direct reports should be the CEO's, if only because he or she has far more information about the person and the business. It can be a tremendous time drain for the CEO to defend every people decision to the board. Fair game is to ask about the rationale for the change, the criteria for selection, and the person's qualifications and growth potential.

The board oversteps if it asks to interview the candidates—unless the job is a stepping stone to the executive suite or is pivotal to company performance. Most boards, for example, are very interested in the CFO. Others have a similar focus on the general counsel, the head of HR, or a senior technology person—whichever jobs the board believes are absolutely critical for the company and the times. For those positions, the CEO will get several directors involved to help clarify what the criteria for the job should be, and possibly to interview two or three final choices. They might also help with the reference-checking process, drawing on their personal networks. That was the case at GE when Bill Conaty was nearing retirement as head of HR. Knowing the critical role HR plays in developing GE's world famous leadership strength, the board was highly engaged in the choice of Conaty's successor. The ultimate decision was still the CEO's, of course.

In most cases, directors will defer to the CEO's judgment in the actual hiring. But boards can also help improve that judgment. When one company's CFO retired, the board worked closely with the CEO to help refine the description of the CFO job in changing external conditions. The CEO was focused on the core accounting skills and managing relationships with existing financing partners as the non-negotiable criteria for the new CFO. But the board suggested that a complete mastery of global financial markets might be needed ("We can always hire good accountants to work with the CFO") and that the CFO must also be a good CEO candidate.

Adjusting the criteria changed the slate of CFO candidates; the previous front-runner wasn't necessarily seen as a potential CEO. When a director suggested a dark-horse candidate in executive session, an up-and-comer who showed enormous promise, it opened the CEO's eyes. "He could run a business three times bigger than the business unit he's running," the director believed. "If we don't move him up, we'll lose him." The board got to know the leader over a period of several months and came to a consensus with the CEO that he should be the next CFO.

Preparing for the Worst

Too often, boards are reticent to address the elephant in the room: emergency succession. Yet for boards to really own up, they have to face the reality that the unexpected can happen. Just as the country's presidency has a strict line of succession, the board must have plans in case of a health emergency or of a CEO leaving for a bigger job. At a minimum, it has to be prepared to name an interim CEO, perhaps from its own ranks, in order to lead the search for a new CEO.

Again, the current CEO has to be involved throughout; the board should give no impression that it is setting up a suc-cession process behind his or her back. But the decision is the board's; directors should not be mollified by a CEO who says, "Don't worry. I have an envelope in my desk with a name in it." And the board should periodically revisit the emergency succes-sion by redefining the non-negotiable criteria and ensuring their emergency name still fits the job requirements.

Key Points

- Boards must be on the offensive to ensure the company has the right CEO at all times. Even a highly successful CEO can become wrong for the company as conditions change.

- A well-designed succession process starts by pinpointing what the company needs most. It also reveals what each candidate really has to offer, shaking loose directors' biases toward or against CEO candidates they already know.

- Discussing succession several years in advance allows time to get to know the candidates well, and if the field falls short, to bring in outsiders below the CEO level.

- Boards should get to know more leaders at lower levels than they typically do, and they must know who will take charge in an emergency.

Question 5.

DOES OUR BOARD REALLY OWN THE COMPANY'S STRATEGY?

The financial crisis of 2008 laid bare a long buried truth: that many boards do not really own the strategy of their company. Evidence had been mounting of boards' failure to ensure that their companies have a clear, credible strategy with appropriate risk levels. Motorola, Yahoo!, Sears, and the Detroit automakers come to mind. But problems in the macroeconomic environment exposed inherent risks in many company strategies that caught their boards off guard.

The ongoing transformation of the external landscape demands a fresh look at strategy. The market values of many businesses and assets have declined beyond belief, and their cash needs have become urgent. It can be hard for management to abandon its old way of thinking and dramatically shift its strategy, but that may be required, and for some, time is quickly running out. One CEO just told her board she is deliberately narrowing the focus and cutting the enterprise by one half in less than a year. These moves are necessary, she said, to remain a going concern. The goal is to survive, manage for cash, retain the right customers, and find enough capital to fund the future while the storm runs its course. Companies have not faced such daunting tasks under such deep and quickly deteriorating circumstances for many decades.

As managements revisit their strategies, boards need to engage more deeply with them on it. A growing number of directors, particularly those joining a board for the first time, will accept nothing less. They will not approve a strategy they don't fully understand. They want to participate in the strategy process, because only then will they understand in some depth the why's and how's of the strategy. They are asking their CEOs to bring strategy issues to the board and reserve half the meeting time for open discussion. "Don't come with a buttoned-down strategy document," they're saying, and "talk to us about the knotty issues you're grappling with; tell us what's on your mind."

For management, this is a complete reversal in their modus operandi. They can no longer dim the lights and say to the board: "You can see from these 200 slides that we've done our homework, and the folks from McKinsey are here to answer any questions you might have in the last ten minutes of the meeting."

A board that gets engaged on strategy is the best help a CEO can have. Directors can open management's eyes to blind spots, raise the imagination to make bold moves, or advise management to pull in its horns when the risks are too high. Management and the board should work together to select the goals, shape the strategic options (including what markets to compete in and how to go about it), challenge the assumptions and the feasibility of execution, and stress-test against the risks.

Boards that are engaged on strategy prove handy when times get tough. Many of the companies that responded early to the financial crisis of 2008 were those where the CEO and the board talked more frequently than ever before and openly about strategy in the midst of the turmoil. But boards should be engaged in strategy under any circumstances. The fact is that the era of holding strategy at arm's length is now over.

Why Does Management Hesitate to Involve the Board on Strategy?

In the past, CEOs and managers have complained that directors don't know enough about the business to add value. "The directors are busy people with short attention spans," one CEO commented. "They don't have the time to really engage with the strategy to a point where I get anything out of them." Not that he spent the time trying.

Another CEO remarked, "Each board member has such a narrow expertise that they always end up dictating orders to my direct reports. That doesn't add value." A third said, "Some directors start to talk strategy, but then they just push whatever idea they just read about in *Harvard Business Review*. We can't go chasing every last management fad." There's some substance to those complaints, but most directors have experiences, deep expertise, or knowledge of cutting-edge tools that can be an advantage if the CEO were more open to it.

CEOs need to adjust their mindset and do the up-front work to help directors grasp the strategy and its external context so they can have meaningful discussions about it. Given the right kind of focused information, the boards of even the largest and most complex companies can grasp the company's strategic issues and add value. Besides, the very fact that directors don't know all the nitty-gritty details of the company's business can be a huge advantage. They can look at things with fresh eyes and from completely different perspectives.

Some CEOs don't want to take the time or go to the trouble to educate the board. That can be remedied by having the board work with management to find efficient ways to get directors up to speed. As CEO and chairman of Verizon, Ivan Seidenberg gave his board brief updates on the external landscape at the opening of every board meeting. Those periodic "lessons" gave the board a sound foundation when it came time to talk about the strategy.

More often, management's concern is more psychological than practical. Some CEOs don't want to expose their thinking for fear that the board will discover holes in the logic and lose respect for them. Others dread the thought of answering questions they haven't prepared for ahead of time. They should realize that the board wants the same thing they want—a bullet-proof analysis of why this strategy is better than any other—and that directors don't expect management to think of everything. The best thinking comes from focused discussion in an informal atmosphere with give-and-take.

The Content of Strategy

Rifts between management and the board are often the result of misunderstandings about the content of the strategy. *Clarity* is the watchword. The strategy must be clear, specific, and simple enough to be communicated in plain language. If it can't be communicated, people won't be able to break it into key tasks and get the message out throughout the organization. It won't be acted on. Clarity is also a test of focus, which many strategies fail. The board should be able to repeat the strategy in clear concise language, including how it will meet the goals the board and management have agreed on, such as meeting the cost of capital relative to the peer group or competition.

No strategy can ever be assessed without considering the goals it is supposed to deliver on, so discussion of goals must go hand in hand with discussion of strategy. The board and management should decide together what the metrics will be and which will have higher priority. Businesses have multiple goals. The mix of goals must be realistic. And no matter what the metrics are for the long term, it will always get down to whether the business, or the combination of businesses in the portfolio, is fundamentally earning the cost of capital and meeting the goals relative to macro conditions, competition, or the chosen peer group.

Management should help the board get a handle on what is happening outside the four walls of the company, and the board should fill in any gaps they detect in management's perception. The *external context* for the business is continually changing, thus rendering strategies obsolete faster than ever. Every strategy has a shelf life, and for most businesses, that shelf life is increasingly short. Detecting when a strategy is nearing its peak and must be renewed is a crucial task for the board. Even CEOs with great track records can miss the next bend in the road, especially during periods of high volatility, and cause irreparable harm to the business. The failure of Bear Stearns in 2008 should have been a wake-up call for investment banks, yet Lehman Brothers couldn't react fast enough to save itself.

Because of externals, the basic formula for money-making can change, as industries from newspapers and recorded music to paper and pharmaceuticals have discovered. Innovations, like Google's search engine and advertising algorithms, can make it impossible to compete if a company is tied to a more traditional model of money-making. Tough questions about how that formula might be changing demand intellectual mettle and will test the courage of the board and the leadership. You didn't have to be a seer to know that Google was turning Internet search into advertising dollars in new and different ways. Yet companies like Microsoft, Yahoo! and AOL, not to mention the print media, all missed that bend in the road and none could successfully compete with Google. More boards need to ask, "What could make the strategy obsolete?" and keep their eyes open for disruptions caused by competitors, technologies, and cross-industry moves.

The external context also involves competitive angles, like what customers think and how competitors are acting. And boards need to keep apprised of the geopolitical, financial (particularly the capital markets), technological, and social trends that affect the business over the short and long terms.

Informed by understanding the external landscape, the board should engage in discussions of strategy at three levels: the company's *portfolio*, the strategies of *business units* and their *functional* capabilities, all within the *external context* for the business. And the board has to be ready to consider not only relatively safe moves but the occasional *strategic bet*.

Within that external context, every company has a *portfolio*—whether of business units, geographies, product lines, technologies, or some other segmentation. Some might be today's cash generators in mature segments, for example, while others might be small but fast-growing cash-consuming ventures. Together, those businesses combine in a portfolio designed to ensure the company's present and future success.

Portfolios must be refreshed by exiting and acquiring businesses with increasing frequency, and boards should be on the alert to help management decide when it's time to change the mix. It's a difficult task to exit a business when times are good—but it's much harder after the value has plummeted. A vigilant company will trade in a profitable product or service line, even while it is still profitable, if its value has peaked; waiting too long can cause a precipitous decline in value. At the same time, boards can help management see when they should add to their portfolios pieces that are in their infancy and can be bought at affordable prices and nurtured into future winners. In 1998, for example, Sharp exited the cathode-ray tube television business and cut investment in the competitive semiconductor sector, while redoubling efforts in emerging LCD technologies. Since then, revenues have nearly doubled and operating profits have tripled. It's now among the world's leaders in a huge market for displays.

Before a company changes its portfolio, there are a handful of key questions to ask: Does the portfolio mix make you more attractive in the capital markets than the peers with whom you compete for investors? Does each segment perform better than its peer group in the eyes of the investment community? Does the portfolio mix achieve its purpose? (Some portfolios are constructed to lower sensitivity to the business cycle, while others use today's cash cows to feed investment in tomorrow's blockbusters.)

Boards and their managements can't stay at the 50,000 foot level. They need to dive deeper into the strategy of *business units* to ensure the strategy is grounded and that management has looked at alternatives, taken on the right level of risk, and is building the right capabilities and applying the right resources—for each and every business unit. For example, a consumer products company that believes the future of its cosmetics business is overseas, notably in India where its brand stands for luxury rather than value, must have the capabilities to grow its presence there, and management must personally be allocating time to that strategically important area.

Each business unit will have its own external context and its own portfolio and positioning issues to go over. From that foundation, boards should ask how margins will change in the face of natural resource price volatility, for example. In some cases they need to learn whether contract terms are changing. They should wonder how market segmentation is changing and explore whether the company should change from an intermediary distribution strategy to serving consumers directly—or vice versa. Discussion should come further down to the *functional* capabilities that are integral to the strategy. Strategies can fail when boards don't do a deep dive into what it takes to execute. Does the company have the leadership and access to capital to carry it out? Does it have the capabilities required? A realistic assessment is needed here. And the board has to know what really differentiates the company from its competitors at a functional and operating level, for different business units. This line of thinking may point to opportunities to pull ahead by building a functional capability, in, say, the supply chain or direct sales, as Dell did. Knowing what that differentiator is allows the board to define a set of indicators to benchmark internal processes—whether production systems, brand equity, or associates' productivity—in order keep track of the company's competitive advantage.

Periodically, the board will need to consider *strategic bets* at any one of the three levels of strategy. Sometimes, it takes bold moves to position a company for the long term, and companies have to be aware of opportunities that could completely reshape the company, even when times are good. In fact, when times are good, the company may be best able to make capital-intensive strategic bets. The launch of the iPod digital music player in 2001 and the iTunes music store in 2003 was a strategic bet at the portfolio level that has paid off handsomely for Apple. Both were completely new markets for the company and there was no way to know whether consumers would embrace the nascent products. Apple made the investments not only to create breakthrough music players and software, but also to combine vital agreements with major music producers with technology to protect copyrights. Without those complementary elements, the strategy would probably not have been so successful. By 2005, 39 percent of the company's revenues came from music-related products.

Strategic bets might also emerge at other levels of strategy. At the business unit level, for instance, deciding to enter a new market that will accelerate growth is a strategic bet. If you view the iPod as a business unit, Apple opening its own retail outlets against the common wisdom was a strategic bet, and a good one. Apple stores have generated record-breaking margins per square foot of retail space. At the functional level, companies might consider building key capabilities—initiatives like vendor-managed inventory or lean manufacturing—that will differentiate the company's operations from its competitors. Forgoing the cost savings in outsourcing functions to build process advantages in-house is a strategic bet.

The board might need to make sure management is at least thinking about strategic bets, at all three levels. Companies might not be able to avoid making the occasional strategic bet, so it pays to be continuously scanning for them, even if they are ultimately rejected. Companies need to agree on how much risk they should take to achieve what strategic goals. The CEO needs to show the risks involved. What are the conditions that will lead to success? What capabilities need to be built? What are some milestones along the way? What will be the likely competitive reaction? What will happen if the bet does not pay off? And what will happen if the bet is not made? All of those questions need to be talked through.

Engaging the Board:
A New Process of Strategy

Boards and managements need to craft a new social process for engaging in the development and choice of strategy. The following process used at two companies is the best practice I have seen so far. This process has five sequential steps spread throughout the fiscal year, all of which must be implemented.

Step 1. Discuss External Trends

The CEO sets the stage for getting the board fully engaged in understanding the changing external environment by presenting his interpretation of data and trends. But the CEO should learn as well as educate. Directors' insights, knowledge, and ability to look at the landscape through a variety of different lenses sharpen and expand management's perceptions and can become an important foundation for creating strategic alternatives and making the final choice of strategy. The diverse backgrounds, different cognitive lenses, and experiences of directors looking at the same phenomenon can help the CEO detect patterns before competitors do. The dialogue stimulates new perceptions and often raises the altitude of imagination and thinking among the operating people.

One of the best ways to continually increase the board's education about the business and its context is to include a thirty to sixty minute discussion about various trends at each board meeting. It helps to also send directors background reading material by outside experts in advance of the session. Even better, invite experts to dinner the night before the board meeting for a Q&A. Boards do a great deal of learning through questions and answers.

Any materials sent to the board ahead of time must be concise and relevant, and the learning should be designed to be cumulative over the six to eight sessions of the fiscal year. As knowledge builds, the board and management come to a common understanding of the external landscape.

Step 2. Capture the Essence of the Strategy in Writing

For debate to be spirited but constructive, all participants need to have a common understanding of the content they are debating. Management can provide this common base by distilling in about five to seven pages or 2000 words the gist of the strategy. It should be written in ordinary language; financials for this first cut can be added as a couple of separate pages.

The document should explain the content of the strategy— "where to play, how to play, and how to win"—and describe what goals the proposed strategy will deliver. It should also state the three to five strategy alternatives that are on the table, the three to five most important opportunities that need to be explored intensively, the most critical competitive threats that are anticipated, the most important risks in the proposed strategy, and how shareholders will view the choice. This document also should articulate the three to five most critical assumptions about the external environment. It need not explain all the myriad trends in the external environment; that will come through the dialogue. All of this must be expressed in crisp, concise language.

The reader will know in less than twenty minutes whether the proposed strategy is clear. Never mind whether it is a good strategy or a bad one or whether the reader agrees with it or not; can it be easily understood and does it have the right altitude? Is it specific enough and yet sufficiently broad? One-liners like "we will take this [high-end specialized product line] to the mass market" demonstrate a clear message but are at too high a level. They don't explain the strategy well enough for directors to get engaged in it. The newly hired CEO of an after-market auto parts retailer presented his strategy that way, emphasizing the shift away from end-consumers to professional mechanics. It was a good strategy and it was clearly stated, but he had to be coached on how to convey more of the strategy's building blocks, like how store layout would change to accommodate the shift.

There should be rigor in the analysis of customer preferences and not an overreliance on financial analysis and growth metrics. The document might say, for example: "We're going to position the company in these five segments. Our primary two segments are generating 80 percent of current revenues, but there's flat growth in both segments because the spending power of customers is linked to a youth population that isn't growing. So we are going to focus on execution by doing the following seven things: . . . In two other segments, we need to ramp up our growth rates overseas, where the brand is strengthening. Specifically, we'll be focusing on these four things: . . . In the last segment, we are still refining the technologies that we believe will create our next big market, and that our competitors are two years behind us on. We're going to focus on these two milestones. . . ."

The CEO should draft the document personally and not delegate it, although he or she will want to work closely with her direct reports. Indeed, a side benefit of this process is that it prods the management team to make sensible trade-offs. In the process, the team tends to gel.

However hard the CEO works on this document, it should not be considered final. It is a catalyst for thinking and a basis of discussion. The idea is to send it to all the directors in advance of the strategy retreat and solicit their reaction. Most board members will take the time to read and think about a carefully crafted five- to seven-page document. They will raise a lot of questions. The CEO should hear those questions from each director individually in a sixty to ninety minute phone conversation or face-to-face visit.

Step 3. Iterate the Strategy with the Board

Discussing the strategy with each director individually makes a big difference in the quality of the discussion and the final product. For one thing, each director has the chance to explore his

ideas and questions without the time pressures of the boardroom. For another, each has the chance to learn about areas not
covered in the document. Third, the director has a lot of time
to reflect on the essence of the strategy; some individuals highly
value the chance for such cerebral activity in quiet moments.
At the same time, these informal interactions build the relationship between the CEO and the director, and greater trust paves
the way for further insights and suggestions.

After soliciting directors' feedback in person or by phone,
the CEO should synthesize all the inputs and redraft the document, then send it out again and follow up with one-on-one
conversation. The process is time consuming for management,
especially the first few times, but it has a high return on the time
spent. There is nothing more important for a CEO than having
the right strategy and right choice of goals, and for the board, the
right strategy is second only to having the right CEO.

Step 4. Conduct a Strategy Immersion Session

So far the discussions have been one-on-one. Information has
begun to flow, and viewpoints that might otherwise be sup-
pressed have been conveyed to the CEO. Every director has par-
ticipated. Now it's time to pull the whole group together to get
totally immersed in the details and issues around strategy for a
solid two days. This is where the board goes beyond individual
contributions to tap the power of the group's *collective wisdom*.
The simultaneous participation generates more creativity than
one-on-one dialogue, as people listen to each other and ideas
get triggered.

At the two-day annual board retreat, the CEO lays out the
strategy and conducts a spirited dialogue, searching for various
viewpoints. But the group does not seek consensus until they
take the next step in the process, which is to pair two management members with two directors and have them probe even
deeper. The small groups of four should sit at separate tables

in the same room and discuss among themselves for about an hour the same three questions: What three things do you like about this strategy? What three things do you not like about this strategy? What three ideas do you propose that the strategy should seriously consider?

Have someone collect the answers to these questions on a computer and display them on a big screen as they are presented for everyone to see. It is better to gather all the answers to the first question before moving on to the second and the third.

By this time the group is likely to be socially cohesive, and the common ground among the answers begins to emerge. Points of contention and issues that the strategy has not addressed become the agenda items for the following twelve months. As this strategy-making process is repeated year after year, the output of the board improves, as does the relationship between the CEO and the board.

Even after going through this process, there are times when the board still is not comfortable about the assumptions underlying the strategy. A new practice is emerging to deal with such cases, which until very recently was taboo. The practice is to seek validation of the assumptions and the strategy by outside experts. I have known and observed two cases in which the board asked the CEO to engage a consulting firm to do the validation. The firm brought superb competitive data and more detail than was previously available. The strategy did not change one iota, but management and the board got a tremendous boost of confidence.

Flexibility of the Strategy

Even after all the hard work of arriving at a strategy the board and management fully support, the strategy cannot be too rigid. Management must have the flexibility to make adjustments in operating decisions and resource allocation, informed by the granularity of the dialogue with the board. This flexibility is a competitive advantage. On the other hand, management cannot unilaterally ignore or defer strategic moves that were agreed on.

Strategy can never be put to rest. Market dynamics won't wait for the timing of your next strategy session. Constant vigilance, particularly of how the external context affects portfolio decisions and strategic bets, is warranted. Some boards are conducting second immersions during the year to keep strategy high on the agenda. Others are examining more granular elements of the strategy, perhaps individual business units or the external context, three or four times per year at board meetings, to keep it fresh in their minds.

Opportunities can arise very quickly and fortune favors those who are ready to move, like Wells Fargo out-maneuvering Citigroup to acquire Wachovia in fall 2008. Periodic reports help assure the board that management is alert to opportunities but is not being impulsive.

Strategy should always be in the back of directors' minds. It helps to have the strategy brief or a two-page sheet of bullet points in the binder for every meeting.

Management's Link with Strategy

There are times when management might push for the strategy it thinks it can execute rather than the one appropriate for the times. But in fact, management often overestimates its ability to execute, particularly when it comes to strategic bets like making a string of acquisitions. So if doubts arise, directors should bring them up in executive session and seek their colleagues' opinions. If peers confirm the concerns, there are several things a board can do, including engaging a consultant or assigning one or two directors to work with management closely to seek out and vet alternative strategies.

If the board and the CEO have lasting substantive differences, they have a choice: stay with the strategy or replace the CEO. Consider that management has a shelf life too, just like the strategy. A good management team that has delivered results under one strategy, like Terry Semel's early tenure at Yahoo!, can become unsuitable for an emerging new strategy as conditions change. It's a courageous decision to remove a successful CEO; personal relationships have been built and elements of doubt may never fully dissolve. But boards increasingly get up the courage when they recognize that time has passed their CEO by.

Key Points

- Directors want to—and must—get engaged in company strategy. The days of buttoned-down one-way presentations from management are over. Directors want to understand the strategy and contribute to it.

- The shelf-life of a strategy is shortening. The board's objectivity and diverse viewpoints can help management detect a bend in the road and peak times to sell a business.

- Management should create a concise strategy document and use an iterative process to solicit feedback on it. One-on-one conversation with individual directors clarifies the strategy and sets the stage for richer group discussions.

- Boards should consider strategy on three levels—portfolio, business unit, and functional—and watch for opportunities to make occasional strategic bets.

- Strategy is never fixed for long. Boards and management must revisit it frequently because the world continuously changes.

Question 6.

HOW CAN WE GET THE INFORMATION WE NEED TO GOVERN WELL?

The quality of the board's *output* depends heavily on the information the board receives. Boards need to take hold of their information and work with management to design its content, presentation, and frequency so the bulk of directors' time and attention goes toward using it, not wading through it. The right information architecture—the right kind of information presented in a way that enables the board to ask insightful, penetrating questions—lifts the focus in the boardroom. It lets directors go beyond the obvious conclusions about whether or not management met its targets last quarter and orients them toward the future, and toward *cause and effect*. It helps them sort through, for example, the four usual causes for performance deviations: shifts in the macro environment, change in the consumer space, shifts in the competitive pattern, and the commission or omission of management actions.

Boards need the right information not only to be effective monitors but also to influence management's behavior and effectiveness. The purpose is not to run the company or micromanage but to make linkages between causal factors and measures of performance in order to help the CEO anticipate, not just look back.

Clearly the tumultuous changes still working their way through the global financial system create unprecedented levels of uncertainty. CEOs face the challenge of a lifetime trying to stay ahead of the curve. The suddenness of the impact of the crisis highlights the need for boards to step up to the plate and help their CEOs address the harsh realities about their business—and to act decisively. To do that, boards have to know what is emerging in the landscape and how it will affect the business in the days, weeks, months, and years to come. They have to know what management is doing to protect against the elevated risks, such as a liquidity crunch, and to balance short-term survival with positioning for the longer-term.

What directors aren't getting they must demand, and soon. They need to have a handle on the balance sheet (including all possible cash commitments to outside parties), on the financial health of customers, suppliers, and partners, on cost, and on every aspect of total enterprise risk. They have to know that management is making necessary reductions and *shifts in resource allocation* with utmost speed. They have to know execution is progressing on plan. But they can't know everything. The skill is to sort out where to focus, and when.

Directors' time of course is scarce, so information must be clear and concise. That will lay the foundation for discussions that probe the underlying issues and spark ideas about what should be done. The dashboards that some boards are now using can help, but they must be carefully designed. In most cases, the actual information on the dashboard needs to change, with more qualitative analysis and better links to forward-looking strategic indicators.

Boards should not be totally dependent on information internal to the corporation. It is imperative for boards in this fast-changing landscape to continue to see the external context through several independent outside lenses. They need to actively and regularly seek outside sources of information to supplement the internal information management presents.

What Information Should the Board Be Looking At?

Although every board's information needs are unique to the company and the time, the basic architecture is similar. Every board should routinely get the following kinds of information:

Financials

Boards already scrutinize their companies' financial reports. But revenues, margins, assets, liabilities, and the rest of the figures in a 10Q all have back stories: if margins are shrinking, is it because parts prices are rising, because customer-service costs are higher, or because the mix of revenues is shifting from higher-margin to lower-margin segments? Boards should get management's analysis of what is driving the numbers and, more important, how management is addressing the root cause of any shortfalls or downward trends. If cash reserves fell, the board should expect management to explain whether it is because of a dip in revenues, lower currency exchange rates, or off-balance-sheet activities, and to discuss the implications—for instance, how the company will finance its bond maturity next year. Is management taking actions to deal with the revenue decline, for example, by cutting general and administrative overhead? Is management on the offensive or defensive? Is it anticipating or just responding?

The audit committee should work with the CFO to design reports geared around the indicators that are important to that company. Cash is surely one of them. Recent events have made liquidity a grave concern. In some cases, sudden lack of liquidity has turned into insolvency. Every board should get frequent updates on where cash is coming from and going to. Reports should illustrate links between the cash line and balance-sheet figures like inventories and receivables that are key not only to the company's strategic positioning but also to its liquidity. Take, for example, a company that has exceptional capital efficiency because of its direct sales model and build-to-order processes. Its ability to keep inventories near zero and thus free up cash and capital gives it a competitive edge. That advantage disappears, however, if inventory starts to build. Inventory is therefore a hugely important measure for that company's board to track.

Nonfinancials

Leading indicators are usually nonfinancial: measures like order backlog, successful products launched, and percentage of new molecules meeting FDA approvals are the ones that tell the board whether the next quarter, the next year, and the next decade will be successful. Thus, any internal process that is critical to doing business should be communicated, along with its connection to the strategy and to financials.

The idea is to spot performance problems before they become earnings or cash shortfalls. This will turn management's attention to them earlier, so that a dip in market share or customer satisfaction now won't become next quarter's or next year's miss. I know one manufacturer in a very low-margin (2.5 percent) industry whose dashboard provides insight into how its vital supply chain operations affect the bottom line and cash usage.

Boards should work closely with their management teams to identify the critical nonfinancial performance drivers. To determine the right indicators, directors have to understand how the business works. Boards that take the time to develop a dashboard can see the linkage between the companies' strategies, the performance drivers, and future financial results—and that deeper understanding stimulates very incisive dialogue in the boardroom.

External Information

The company does not exist in a vacuum, so externals need to be incorporated in the board's information architecture in three ways. Boards need a clear and concise view of these areas to ensure the next crisis does not sneak up on them.

First, everything is relative, so almost all financial and non-financial information should be benchmarked. A margin boost from 26 percent to 31 percent may not be reason to cheer, for example, if your main competitor's margin is 44 percent. And during a severe downturn, performance might be assessed by comparing whether your company's revenues fell more or less than competitors'. I know one private equity firm that goes to the ends of the earth to benchmark one of its portfolio companies, a major parts supplier to the U.S.–based original equipment manufacturers. It receives information on its pricing at least once a quarter because U.S.–based OEMs are notorious for badgering suppliers for price reductions. It spares no expense in getting the right comparisons for its metrics. When public pure-play competitors are absent, it commissions external studies of business units and private companies to set and rationalize its targets.

Second, the board has to be up-to-date on how competition is evolving. Market share is a common metric, but there's more to consider. If a company's brand sets it apart from competitors, for example, it better track the strength of the brand and the investments that competitors are making in their brands. One retailer's board tracks the effectiveness of its advertising over time to get a sense for how its brand is translating into sales in key markets.

More fundamentally, boards need to see how new entrants and new technologies could threaten the fundamentals of how money is made in the industry, like the disruptions that have ravaged the business models of newspapers and music producers. Google might move fast, as with its Android mobile handset platform. But markets didn't change overnight. Mobile operators and handset makers should monitor how potential disruptions like those are being adopted by customers and partner firms.

In 2008, capital markets began to undergo seismic change at high speed. Investors changed their asset allocation criteria.

The flight to quality began, and fear on the street was palpable. The board needs to recognize changes like this and what is causing the problem. Directors need to know how different avenues of financing are evolving, which ones will remain open, and which ones could get gummed up. Investor and creditor sentiment over mechanisms like revolving lines of credit, auction-rate securities, and asset-backed bonds can freeze up very quickly. No board can afford to dismiss the capital markets viewpoint. In several cases, forward-looking boards got their managements to get money in the bank from their revolving lines of credit in the early part of 2008, even though they did not need the cash at that time.

Third, despite the unprecedented level of uncertainty, boards should have a view on how macro trends are affecting the company and the industry. They might consider any number of trends, from raw materials prices and technology developments to geopolitical updates and macroeconomic forecasts. Whatever the trend, the board should not only hear what's happening in the world, but also gain insights on how the company's strategy might play out under different scenarios. If demand drops by 30 percent, for example, how will it affect your cash flow and operating margins, credit ratings, mark to market valuations, and refinancing? For example, a few companies highly dependent on the European automotive OEMs lost 20 percent of revenue in the fall of 2008, and the domino effect on their finances was wrenching. Some directors were very remorseful that they did not aggressively advise management to stop share buy-backs. Board and management can design the dashboard in a way that can illustrate how the company is stress testing against adverse conditions, including the worst case, such as a severe and protracted economic slowdown combined with a possible late-stage upturn in inflation.

Providing information in all three areas could require significant investments of time and resources from management. Tracking external benchmarks and compiling research on externals involves culling and validating research from many different external sources. Still, for those items that are truly important to the company's success, the board should insist that management periodically commit resources to them.

Milestones

Every company embarks on projects that are vital to long-term competitiveness. Yet projects such as merger integrations must have short-term benchmarks, and those are things the board must ask management to lay out. One industrial firm set out to cut by one-third its order-to-cash cycle, for example, which was near the industry average of 216 days. It expects to take a couple of years to achieve that goal, yet the CFO has quarterly milestones and reports to the board on how improvements are affecting inventories and receivables. Boards might also want to revisit the type of information they get about those projects. The timing of projected cash investment and inflows, for instance, might be just as important as the project's ROI.

Boards should establish milestones to track the effectiveness of the strategy. For a company whose new strategy includes selling to more national versus regional accounts, for example, the board might want to track what percentage of the sales force has received training in the new sales techniques, and how much revenue is coming from each of the targeted national accounts compared with projections.

People

Lastly, boards should get information on the human resources of the company. Are the right people in place to meet the current challenges? Is the company attracting and retaining talent and keeping people motivated? What are the retention levels at the associate level, what is the loss of key talent, particularly from leadership positions, and how are people progressing through the leadership pipeline? They need to track how the talent markets view the company at different points of the leadership pipeline from potential new associates to seasoned managers. Is the company seen as a good employer? Are recruiters noticing different priorities among new generations of workers? The head of human resources should be tapped to provide those answers in management's reports.

The Information Architecture in Practice

Some boards are nominating one or two directors to work with management to re-architect the information flows, usually using dashboards. They work carefully with the CFO—along with the CEO, and the heads of human resources and investor relations, if needed—to agree on the structure and presentation of reports and define the data and information to report. Other directors can express their concerns before the information is redesigned.

The dashboard could be five pages or double that, whatever it takes. Some boards update dashboards monthly and make them available online, which makes the logistics more efficient. In times of crisis, some information might be delivered to the board weekly or even daily.

Dashboards should be consistent in design from month-to-month (or whatever the frequency). But it's vital that there is room and flexibility for management to provide commentary where it is needed. Management shouldn't just update a series of tables—it has to assist the board by interpreting the information. Deviations from plan should be highlighted, as should patterns of change that represent trends and not month-to-month noise in the data. The management team should provide a precise and insightful *narrative* to discuss the root causes of the outliers, as well as action items. Is this a blip in performance or does it portend a rough road ahead? Management's discussion will begin to answer those questions. If a big bump in receivables can be attributed to a single large customer, or a surge in foot traffic is attributable to a significant weather event, say so, along with what management will do to address it.

Then the board can bring its intellectual power to bear. It doesn't have to wait for the next board meeting. When an important unforeseen event takes place, some companies welcome having directors discuss it with management on a conference call between board meetings. This is when the board can shine, bringing different lenses to look at the landscape and how it is affecting the company and its strategy.

If that's not happening on conference calls or in the boardroom, then the board should ask in an executive session whether there is anything it can do to improve the information architecture. And boards should question in their self-evaluations whether their information flow is optimized.

Pay attention to the ambience, too, when management presents information to the board. Using flip charts instead of PowerPoint slides, for instance, creates an informal atmosphere conducive to brainstorming and discussion. Directors are more likely to get engaged, contribute spontaneously, and ask for clarification on the spot. One CEO I know used flip charts to lay out the company's moneymaking in contemporary circumstances, sparking a lively two-and-a-half-hour discussion. That kind of engagement doesn't often occur in a one-way presentation in a darkened room.

Bring the Outside In

Managements can be too internally oriented and may have too narrow an aperture to view the world. Boards need to be continually updated in their view of the changes happening externally, and from multiple angles. They need to regularly seek information and viewpoints from outside sources. In several industrial companies, forward-looking boards and their managements invited speakers such as the president of the New York Fed to meet with the board for a two-hour discussion. Those sessions are invariably eye-opening.

Investment bankers and strategy consultants are common voices in boardrooms. But information from external sources could also come from sources the board may not have considered in the past, like policymakers and think-tank fellows. The idea is for the board and the management team to hear insights and judgments directly from experts. If you were on the board of Ford or General Motors, for example, wouldn't you be interested to know from independent sources how consumer behavior is changing in different segments of Americans because of the credit-crunch? Your interaction on those subjects could help management see the phenomenon from different angles, and help uncover wrong assumptions that could be detrimental to the company's survival.

The management team has to be involved in commissioning presentations like that; management will benefit greatly from such studies and discussions as well. Special presentations are usually made to the board and the management team at dinners before meetings. They often spark rich informal conversations about long-term trends and stimulate directors to think strategically and creatively.

The board would also be well served to have their own internal information sources when assessing leadership and the culture of the organization. Some companies use "pulse surveys" that sample employees periodically to get a flavor of what employees are thinking. I also encourage directors to visit plants and stores to get to know managers and associates up and down the company. Employees might be guarded initially, but they open up when directors ask for their opinions and talk with them. Those interactions give directors a better sense of how the company really operates and the quality of the company's employees in general. Some audit committee members make a point to visit with the finance department for a day before board meetings, and include some informal interactions to make it clear that their proverbial door is always open. A few audit committee members also visit operating department heads or even lower-level managers where key operating decisions are made, because many problems in audit emanate from there.

One controversial best practice that is taking hold given the failures of Enron and WorldCom is for directors to interact with direct reports via small group dinners the night before the board meeting, specifically to get a feel for the culture at the top management level. They can gauge the top management leadership style and how it is changing in times of stress or jubilation. In some cases I have known, the governance committee came to know that the CEO was spending too much time on outside activities and asked him to consider curtailing those activities. By breaking down the barriers between the board and employees, boards also keep their ears open to those rare reports from whistleblowers. It has to be made clear to everyone in the company that whistleblowers who report unethical behavior either at the institutional level or the level of top managers not only will be given due consideration but also will be respected whether the allegations turn out to be true or false. When the board has a more visible, if only occasional, presence throughout the organization, whistleblowers will be more comfortable coming forward. This is not a trivial consideration—as so many shareholders can attest over the past ten years.

Key Points

- Boards should assign one or two directors to work with management on the architecture of the information that comes to directors, because the board needs the right information at the right time.

- Information has to go beyond reporting past performance to show the drivers of future performance. Supplement financial reports with information on company nonfinancials, externals, special projects, and people.

- Management should highlight key figures and include insightful and useful commentary for the board.

- Boards should not get all their information from management alone. They should be more active in seeking outside voices and judgments and hearing directly from employees.

Question 7.

HOW CAN OUR BOARD GET CEO COMPENSATION RIGHT?

When it comes to CEO compensation, the game has changed permanently. The ground rules are being completely rewritten: the volatility of stock prices has driven some options-based incentive pay to zero, competitive shifts are remapping the global economy, and the idea of rigidly comparing performance against traditional competitors is null and void when a significant number of your peers have disappeared or are on the verge of going out of business.

In these conditions, tweaking formulas to avoid criticism over rewards that are not linked to performance simply will not do. Compensation plans must stay relevant and keep management focused on building and protecting shareholder value. To do that, boards need to start with a blank slate and fresh thinking.

Compensation committees will have to take the lead. Their members need to think through how the targets will be determined in the context of the global financial crisis and beyond, what the ideal balance of short-term and long-term targets will be, and what forms of compensation are best to use. They have to dig into the details and help the full board understand the new drivers of the business and what the leader can actually control that will affect the company's short- and long-term success. They also have to wrestle with the mix of fixed and variable pay, given that the market value of equity grants is not only very volatile but also less subject to management control than the company's intrinsic performance.

The competitive landscape is dynamic, and boards must come to grips with how to adapt as events unfold. Every management team must make mid-course adjustments during a quarter or a year. The board has to decide if those course corrections have made the company stronger, and reserve the right to adjust the targets and the final amount. Flexibility is important, but those decisions can't be arbitrary or they will open the door to criticism. Boards should set guidelines for how the board will exercise judgment in a way that is transparent to both management and investors. CEO compensation must stand up to societal scrutiny.

Executive compensation demands tremendous time and dedication. Jack Mollen, executive VP of human resources of EMC Corp., said his company's compensation committee met sixteen times in 2007, and that's not including regular conference calls. More compensation committees should follow that lead, roll up their sleeves, and get to work. And they cannot turn the work over to compensation consultants, any more than audit committees can delegate their responsibility to outside auditors as they did in the past.

Determining What Performance You Are Paying For

Mechanical formulas and quantitative absolutes simply don't work, because by generalizing across businesses and industries at a fixed moment in time, they freeze management's incentives. A "set and forget" approach to compensation ignores the fact that conditions will change. The right way to approach the compensation plan is for the board to scrap the static absolutes, figure out what's really driving the business, and use its collective judgments over the course of the year to evaluate what the CEO and his team accomplished.

This is a job for the board, not for compensation consultants. The compensation committee should be thoughtful and specific about the performance measures that will make a difference, and the whole board should discuss them with an internal team consisting of the CEO, the CFO, and the head of human resources. The idea is to identify a handful of targets that capture the building blocks of the business, and in some cases to prioritize them.

Using a single measure, even a sophisticated one like economic value-added (EVA), can't be relied upon. Rather, a mix of short- and long-term objectives is necessary, and they shouldn't all be P&L accounting measures, like ROI, revenue growth, EBITDA, and the like. Those measures miss the risks that could become evident at a later date, a phenomenon we witnessed in most investment banks and even AAA-rated insurance companies during the financial meltdown. So measures should reference the risks that are captured on the balance sheet, possibly including operational items like inventories and accounts receivable, or financial items like liquidity risk. And they should acknowledge risk factors that don't lend themselves well to quantification, thus allowing the board to exercise its judgment on whether management achieved its goals with appropriate risk. Almost all risks appear with a time lag from the time the action is taken or decision is made to the time the risks actually materialize and come to haunt the business.

Some of the objectives might also be nonfinancial in nature. A growth company might care about innovation or branding, for example, and a company in turnaround might look at progress toward economic profit down the road, even if it is still not earning its cost of capital at the time. Objectives that capture whether the company's strategy will later lead to good financial results have to be part of the equation; this will prevent CEOs from cutting promising R&D programs in order to make their EBITDA targets, for example.

There is a tendency to focus on total shareholder return as a tangible way to measure CEO performance over the long term, but it's an imperfect measure. Quantitative targets over a horizon of several years can be problematic, because all it takes is one sharp movement in the general stock market to render them meaningless. An alternative is to break down long-term building blocks into actions and related investments that are executed systematically year after year. Brand-building or leadership development efforts, for example, take many years of diligent investment to yield long-term value. But some advertising programs can measure improvements to the brand over the course of a year. Annual recruitment and retention performance can measure the effectiveness of longer term leadership development programs aimed at building superior bench strength for key jobs.

The board should also stress-test the goals against volatile external factors, including commodities prices, the economy, and the stock market. The compensation committee should have detailed discussions with management on the likelihood of hitting the specific targets—and the circumstances that would have to be present in order to hit them. Would it depend on energy prices staying within a certain band? Would it depend on expansion of a major customer's business? Are those assumptions unrealistic? Make sure the committee factors that in when it sets objectives. Many companies set stretch targets for short-term objectives that could double a base package for the top team. That might be too high. *Targets that are unrealistic or too far outside of management's control won't convince the executive team to work harder; they'll convince management to do dumb things.* We have seen enough of this among financial institutions leading up to the financial crisis. Any assignment of highly ambitious targets must be based on discussion of what it will take to accomplish them.

Balancing Fixed and Variable Pay

Boards should match cash incentives to shorter term objectives and equity awards to longer term objectives. This is an important linkage that will connect the operating performance with bonuses and also relate long-term building blocks with equity or options grants that vest over a long period.

The tricky part is figuring out the right balance between fixed and variable elements of the package. Current practice seems to involve about 20 percent of total compensation in fixed annual salary and another 25 percent in an annual bonus, both in cash. The rest of a typical package is equity-based, in various combinations of options, restricted stock, and the like, applied with plenty of imagination and no limits to the upside. *Many boards accept this structure without considering it in the context of the new external realities.* They hold to the belief that this is conventional practice, and consultants recommend it across all industries. Is the variable component too high? The board should make a judgment and not automatically follow some general practice.

Variable pay awards linked to equity grants are subject to the vagaries of stock valuations, the incompetence of Wall Street analysts, the herd effect among investors (as in the dotcom bubble), and the uncontrollable dynamics of the global financial system. Great companies, even those with rising revenues and solid credit ratings, can watch their stock prices drop simply because an industry falls out of favor on Wall Street, rather than because of anything management has done. Even a respectable rise in earnings might not be enough to offset an industrywide P/E ratio that falls from 30 to, say, 13. And poor-performing companies can rise with the tide of a bull market or the industry P/E ratio, thus rewarding CEOs who haven't delivered.

Too much emphasis on equity awards has even forced boards to reprice options in order to keep their equity awards relevant, which is not a good practice. Indeed, options valuation is a potential quagmire; a dollar figure results from a black-box calculation using a host of assumptions that even investment banks often get wrong. If a board is relying on Black-Scholes to calculate potential awards, it had better know the formula inside and out. Otherwise, sticking with restricted stock might be advisable.

Accepted wisdom calls for equity awards because they align managers' interests with those of shareholders. While there is some truth to that, the philosophy needs to be moderated. Managers with high equity awards are more exposed to stock price movements than shareholders. Shareholders can hedge, diversify, or find other ways to manage investment risk, while management of course cannot diversify the source of its pay-check, nor can it sell or hedge its holdings at will. The board also needs to deal with the "long-term interest" premise. Market corrections can take a long time, and by the time they do occur, the business environment may have vastly changed.

Using Your Judgment

A slavish following of quantitative measures will not do justice to the board's hard work in aligning compensation with strategic goals. In almost all cases, the board needs the latitude to exercise judgment when evaluating CEOs to make allowances for events beyond management's control. Business cycles change, and macro events like hurricanes or political turmoil happen. The sun does not rise on January 1 and set on December 31; boards should be evaluating everything the CEO did or didn't do in between.

Case in point was one CEO who had an opportunity to make a compensation target related to earnings growth by selling an important asset at the bottom of the market. He chose not to sell the asset, a wise decision considering not only the market conditions, but also the asset's role in the company's long-term plans. The full board agreed with the move, but the compensation committee didn't acknowledge the CEO's decision and denied the full bonus. What message did that send to the management team?

One way to keep the compensation plan flexible is to assign new targets quarterly. EMC, whose revenue comes almost entirely from products that are less than eighteen months old, sets new targets on a conference call every quarter as one component of its executive compensation. The targets run the gamut of categories: financial, merger integration, innovation, talent management, diversity and sustainability, recapitalization plan, and so forth. The EMC board then has the flexibility to adapt to circumstances as the year unfolds.

Judgments can't be made arbitrarily, however. The board should examine changes in external conditions, and the management team's response to them. For example, in a time when oil price volatility is having a major impact on many companies' cost structures, a board might first analyze the link between it and the performance target, say margins, and consider what the results would have looked like if the price of oil had stayed constant. That takes both judgment and analytical skills.

Then, the board might consider the steps management took to deal with the change in oil prices. Did management buy hedges that will reduce volatility going forward? Or did management cut its advertising expenditures in order to make the numbers this year, thus adversely affecting the brand effectiveness? Boards should hear out the CEO's case. When management knows the board will be considering those types of trade-offs, it is more likely to make the right decisions.

Mixing analytics and judgment is controversial in some quarters. A distrustful public believes that more discretion for boards leads to higher pay. Because of this risk, many boards shy away from giving the wrong impression. But courage is important.

To be consistent in exercising its judgment, the board should develop and articulate a clear philosophy and framework for top management compensation. The purpose of a philosophy is to clearly describe the board's overall intent by stating in clear terms what the board will and will not do. The philosophy should be flexible enough to adapt to changes in the external environment and yet meet the test of consistency over time. Compensation should be fair and equitable, competitive, motivational, balanced between the short and long term, and aligned with shareholders' interests. But the philosophy should go beyond this boilerplate to state, for instance, the areas in which the board will exercise discretion instead of being bound by formulaic or absolute numerical targets.

The philosophy might state, for example, that compensation will lie in the 50th percentile of the competitive set; that given the company's condition and its industry context, the ratio of fixed cash compensation to equity will be 40/60 over the long-range plan; that compensation will never be more than five times salary; and that it will be adjusted for tailwinds (for example, when the P/E ratio of the whole market goes up and gives management a free ride) and headwinds (when the P/E ratio for the whole market goes down and penalizes management). The philosophy might state that shareholders are expected to bear a great deal of responsibility for the macro factors that are beyond the control of any manager. It might also state that management will bear responsibility for the long-term risks inherent in short-term decisions; this can be accomplished, for instance, by awarding one-fifth of the equity every year with the board's option to withhold the remaining portion.

A compensation philosophy is where the board also can articulate the distinction between shareholder value and shareholder interests. Four or five consecutive years of decision making aimed at maximizing shareholder value (typically calculated as absolute appreciation in the stock price plus dividends) can send the company over a cliff and work against shareholder interests. History provides many examples. Therefore, the philosophy might say that the company's mission is to build the intrinsic value of the company over time rather than to maximize shareholder value. It is well known that at a given point in time there can be a discrepancy between a company's real intrinsic value and the actual pricing of that value in the stock market. The board can reserve the right to make a judgment about how to deal with that discrepancy by considering activities that impact intrinsic value negatively or positively, such as improving (or damaging) the company's reputation or working with local communities or national legislators more (or less) effectively. The board can state its willingness, for instance, to tolerate investment that reduces shareholder value in the short term but builds value for the future.

A compensation framework translates the philosophy into specifics year by year as external conditions change. The framework should address the following items at a minimum:

- **Management performance relative to direct competition.** Every company has more than one metric for judging top management performance. The framework should state which ones matter and which combination the board will use to show that management has done better than a peer group of *direct competitors*. Did management achieve better margins and/or better revenue growth through its initiatives like marketing or product launches compared with direct competitors? Did it continue to increase the gap between itself and the competition in productivity, as Toyota has done? The board must exercise judgment in a given year or even quarter to stay in tune with the environment.

- **Management performance in the context of uncontrollable macro factors.** The framework should include a methodology for taking uncontrollable factors into account in determining management's progress toward targets. The board should make a judgment relative to the direct competition about how well management performed in the context of uncontrollable factors, such as politics, acts of god, terrorism, the idiosyncrasies of the capital markets, or a seismic shift in the macro economy (for instance, the sudden blockage of liquidity and credit availability in late 2008).

- **Point targets versus a range.** Targets should be set in collaboration with management based on shared assumptions about the future macro and competitive factors. Because macro factors have become so complex, volatile, and uncontrollable in the short run, the board should have a range of targets that can be adjusted based on critical factors.

As long as boards are transparent about their basic approach to compensation and are diligent in applying it, respected analysts like the Corporate Library will support the board and allow it to exercise judgment responsibly.

Working with Compensation Consultants

Compensation consultants are a valuable part of the compensation process, but they are an input to, not a substitute for, the board's deliberations. The board itself has to own up to the outputs, including defining and prioritizing the objectives that link the strategy to management's incentives and the judgments that determine management's awards. Where consultants shine is providing external data to help the board's deliberations along the way.

Consultants provide a lot of great information to boards on the range and median of compensation packages and on their architecture, including the mix of fixed and variable pay. They can also share practices other boards use to construct their targets and structure awards. But boards need to have hard and detailed conversations on their own and be prepared to push back at consultants if necessary.

Take assembling peer groups, for example, on which consultants do a lot of work. Peers need to be selected with more care than what many companies are doing right now—and it's the committees that need to take the reins. I heard one consultant make the case to add a high-margin cosmetics company that is expanding overseas to the peer group for a much larger, low-margin food and beverage company in turnaround. That made no sense at all. The consultant's argument was that they raid each other's talent. Is that really true? And if so, at what level—vice president or lower level?

First of all, boards need to understand what the peer group is being used for. Is it to gauge overall competitiveness, growth, or the ability to attract top talent or to compete for investment capital? Those four purposes might point to a different peer group for each. EMC, for example, uses one set of peers to set operating targets such as revenue growth (including non-U.S. companies and private companies to define the product markets in which EMC competes), a second set to benchmark compensation (including only public high-tech U.S. companies to represent the companies EMC competes with for talent), and a third set of peers to judge external conditions. All three peer groups serve a unique purpose in the overall compensation plan.

Then there needs to be robust discussion of the criteria for selecting peers. Direct competitors are almost always included. But including non-direct competitors presents tricky choices. Should a freight railroad like CSX include airlines in the competitors' peer group? Both are cyclical businesses in the larger transportation sector, with exposures to volatile fossil fuel prices. But there is little competition between them and, in any case, the airlines are a structurally defective industry. It's a tough call.

The committee should also consider what is behind the performance of peers. How many companies realized having Enron in their compensation peer group was a big mistake until the company's shortcomings were uncovered? Some boards unknowingly incented their management teams to compete with a fraudulent company in order to make their bonuses. Management might have insights about whether a company should be included; I know one CEO who didn't want Enron in his peer group because he was certain something was wrong with the business model.

Those types of debates should play out as compensation committees choose peers that are appropriate, not just convenient. There will always be some give and take as consultants make suggestions and the committee debates which ones are a better fit. And consultants can help by providing data on the peers and by crunching performance for potential peers over a long time to test hypotheses.

Keeping a Strong CEO-Board Relationship

Of all the topics in the boardroom, CEO compensation has the most potential to create tension in the board-management relationship. It's a negotiation, after all. This puts compensation committee chairs in a particularly influential and sensitive role. If they take a stance too hard, it can demotivate a CEO. There have been many awkward moments, to put it politely, between CEOs and comp committee chairs.

One board rotated a terrific retired executive who was an independent director, I'll call him "Charlie," as chair of the compensation committee. Charlie worked hard to get up to speed, working primarily with a compensation consultant that he had worked with on a previous board. Then Charlie and the CEO sat down with the consultant. Almost right away, the consultant came across as dogmatic, firmly disagreeing with the CEO on many points. One issue at stake was the peer group, which the CEO felt was filled with companies at a different stage of growth. The CEO pushed back but Charlie deferred to the consultant. The CEO left the meeting frustrated.

In this case, the Lead Director later picked up on the tensions and stepped in to defuse the situation. He later described to me three lessons he learned. For one thing, the rest of the compensation committee had to get more involved. Too many boards are leaving the chair of the compensation committee to do all the heavy lifting. Second, the chair of the compensation committee has to be aware of the fact that tension in the compensation discussions could affect behavior, so picking a committee chair with the right temperament is crucial. Third, consultants should be vetted more carefully by the committee. In that case, the consultant gave the clear impression that he was fishing for human resources work from the company, in addition to delivering services for the board. That's not acceptable.

Every once in a while, however, a board may have to stand up to a CEO and do the right thing for the company. Chief executives have to accept the possibility that their variable pay may drop if a recession hits, as happened in 2008, and they need to be honest about it. That means no excuses. I heard one chief executive blame rising oil prices for her underperformance, when she could have hedged or mitigated the risk. Another CEO blamed skyrocketing raw materials prices for falling margins in 2007, when that management team failed to push through the appropriate price increases that competitors were able to achieve. Those boards used their judgment and saw through the excuses.

If the excuses keep coming and the CEO is hanging on to every last dollar despite the board's judgments, directors have to accept that they might need to part company with the chief over pay. It's happened at several prominent companies. Nobody is indispensable (except possibly during emergencies, and even then only for the short term). There is almost always more than one person who could be a good CEO. Recently, I heard of a search committee that ruled out a highly respected external successor early on, solely because the price tag was too high. That's a board that thinks like an owner.

Some CEOs have tried to use joining a private equity funded company as negotiating leverage. However, private equity CEOs usually invest a huge amount of personal wealth in the ventures. And private equity's compensation plans are unmistakably linked to long-term performance; CEOs will make a ton of money only if they deliver. If they leave or are terminated early, they forfeit a lot of upside. And the vagaries of the capital markets pose a risk in private equity, too, sometimes making it hard to realize the value of the business. Private equity may add more intensity to the competition for some CEOs, particularly veteran cost cutters, but not enough to justify outrageous pay packages for all.

Monitoring Societal Pressures

In fall 2008, as the federal government worked on a rescue plan for the worst financial crisis since the Great Depression, what was the top concern of citizens on Main Street? Limiting

CEO pay for struggling financial firms. That should be a real eye-opener.

When it comes to societal pressures, boards have to understand which way the wind is blowing. Pay is under the microscope, and fighting public sentiment is a good way to erode a company's reputation. Sentiment backing "say on pay," for example, is gaining momentum; at some point, boards may need to adopt principles that give weight to shareholder views on compensation plans.

To ease societal pressures, it helps to make compensation, including every last perk, completely transparent (which doesn't mean hiding details in footnotes). Shareholders need to know where their money is going and for what reason. Going further and making the deliberations transparent will demonstrate to shareholders that the CEO's pay is in line with the company's strategy and its performance. As long as that is clear, boards will be given the leeway to exercise judgment and ensure the compensation plan motivates the right behaviors.

Boards can't formulate pay packages that will both incent the right behaviors and satisfy every last critic, but they need to avoid the most contentious practices. Right now, the typical overall pay package is not what raises activists' hackles the most. Instead, critics are most concerned about outliers, adjustments of awards, and severance. Let's take those one at a time.

Compensation outliers are usually created by boards that don't think through the possibilities of tailwinds and bull markets. In one case, a board made 88 percent of a CEO's potential compensation variable, tied directly to the stock price, in a bull market. It did not have a philosophy and it did not have the courage to exercise judgment in its equity award.

When the CEO sold the energy services company after a few years, just below the market peak, he earned a payout in the mid-nine figures. But he hadn't really achieved very much other than take advantage of rising oil prices in a bull market for energy stocks. Boards have to be more aware of and sensitive to the total potential compensation in absolute terms and in terms relative to other employees. Make no mistake: outliers will be singled out in public. A few directors have been forced to resign from their boards because they were deemed to be in the pockets of these outliers' CEOs. Appearances matter.

Adjustments of awards are usually pushed by CEOs against boards that don't show enough courage. CEO Kerry Killinger built Washington Mutual with little respect for risk. At the start of the housing bust that initiated the financial crisis in 2008, he had the gall to ask his board to ignore the company's mortgage-related losses when calculating profits that factor into executive bonuses going forward. Needless to say, the chair of the compensation committee came under heavy fire for agreeing to the deal at the annual meeting in April 2008.

Severance has been where boards have come under the most intense criticism, notably, for nine-figure golden parachutes for chief executives who have failed. The issue is only intensifying after payouts to CEOs like Stanley O'Neal, who left Merrill Lynch after announcing a $2.24 billion quarterly loss in 2007 yet received $161.5 million in equity awards and retirement benefits.

These headline-makers are often the result of lopsided deals struck when the board is forced to recruit a CEO from outside. And that decision can become an embarrassment if the CEO doesn't work out. Merrill's experience underscores the problem. To hire John Thain from NYSE Euronext as a replacement for O'Neal, Merrill had to offer him substantial compensation for giving up awards from the NYSE.

It helps if the board makes the potential severance transparent at the time of the appointment, as Merrill did with Thain. It allows the public to see at the outset that the board is not hiding anything. Even still, boards might need to show more of a spine in granting severance packages. Payouts like O'Neal's often involve unvested equity awards. While some employment contracts call for equity awards to vest upon termination for any reason (an invitation for public outrage), others allow the board to decide how those awards will vest. Should the CEO be let go, boards will need to withhold a greater portion of those awards. It's a difficult negotiation given that the CEO is likely going to fight for every last share. But it's a necessary one to demonstrate the board is acting like an owner.

If boards don't grasp the reins and do their job on compensation, shareholders will let them know. "Dealing with shareholders' money, . . . [directors] should behave as they would were it their own," Warren Buffett wrote in his 2002 letter to shareholders. If boards don't behave as representatives of shareholders, the real owners are going to step up. And they are increasingly using compensation practices as a litmus test of whether the board is owning up.

Key Points

- Boards have to get comfortable making judgments about executive compensation. Rigid formulas and absolute numerical targets don't always work as expected, especially given the volatility in the global financial markets.

- Boards have to rethink how much pay should be at risk, what factors the CEO can really control, and what companies should be in the peer group for what purpose.

- The full board, not one or two individuals, should determine CEO compensation.

- A "compensation philosophy" makes the guidelines for decision making explicit, while reserving the board's right to exercise discretion. Most constituencies accept the board's judgment provided the decisions are thoughtful and the guidelines transparent.

- Compensation committees have to step up their efforts to dig into the details of executive compensation; they cannot delegate the job, even to the best consultants.

Question 8.

WHY DO WE NEED A LEAD DIRECTOR ANYWAY?

Some directors say their board doesn't really need a leader. They and their colleagues get along just fine, and besides, no individual director has authority over any other.

I have a different view. No group of people, be it an orchestra, a basketball team, or a project team, ever becomes high-performing without a clear leader, and boards are no exception. I have seen too many boards become factionalized, unfocused, and indecisive because no one kept the dialogue on track, surfaced underlying conflicts, or pushed the group to reach consensus. The best boards have leaders who do all those things, shaping the social dynamics of the board both inside and outside the boardroom, facilitating convergence of individual directors' viewpoints, and facilitating communication and understanding between management and the board.

This type of leadership, usually coming from a Lead Director or nonexecutive chair, is different from most other leadership positions. It's subtle and respectful and based on trust instead of formal power. Exercised properly, it takes the board to higher ground, and thus the leader earns tremendous respect among her peers.

The choice of leader has a tremendous impact on the board's ability to function as a group and govern well. Boards should therefore develop a clear view of what they expect their Lead Director to do and a clear process for assigning the role. They should select a Lead Director from among their ranks who has the temperament, personality, and skills to build positive board dynamics in and outside the boardroom. That person should have no greater influence on board decisions than any other director. He or she should, however, enhance the board's ability to make those decisions as a group in a way that is timely and intellectually honest and taps the wisdom and experience of every board member.

How Board Dynamics Affect Governance

Since no individual director alone can make a decision and all decisions have to be group decisions, board dynamics are a huge determinant of whether a *board adds or destroys value*. As the power balance has been shifting away from the CEO, directors have felt empowered to speak their minds. They have begun to dive deeper into corporate affairs and no longer hesitate to question the CEO in depth. For the most part, this trend is positive. But in some cases directors become so contentious toward management that dialogue becomes cross-examination, stifling give-and-take, or they become so rigid that they cannot reach consensus among their peers.

It's well known that boards can commit sins of omission, standing idle as the company takes a downward slide. Sometimes a board falls short because an "untalkable issue" never surfaces; one or two directors are aware of it, but it doesn't get expressed because of the unwritten rules of the board's social dynamics, so it doesn't get addressed. Remember, a board is a social group, much like any other. Its social dynamic can be unconsciously shaped by the behaviors of one or a few influential individuals.

Following the merger of two telecom companies, the turnover of new subscribers became very high, causing a liquidity problem and making it hard to service the merged company's high debt load. Outsiders began to grumble that the technologies of the two companies were incompatible, and as the company continued to struggle, the stock price dropped precipitously. The newly combined board was on its way to committing a sin of omission until an investor joined. He put the issues of incompatible technologies and misallocation of capital on the table.

Once those issues were brought to light, the board took hold of them. They brought in a new CEO, who sought advice from Wall Street investment bankers to fix the liquidity and future financing issues. Surely someone on that board had an inkling that the company's integration problems were making the debt load unbearable before the new director spoke up, but for some reason, that viewpoint wasn't articulated.

Sins of commission are equally damaging. Removing a good CEO because of interpersonal issues between a key director and the CEO, for example, can destroy tremendous value. These misjudgments are more likely to occur when debate is limited and only a few voices dominate.

A CEO who was performing well against the company's peers lost his job under such a scenario. He became vulnerable when the highly influential senior-most director who had been his ardent supporter retired from the board. As a result, the board's power balance fell to two new directors. One of the new directors, who had a consulting background, was highly analytic. The CEO was not. The chief executive had good business judgment, and indications were that the strategy change he was implementing was working, but he did not present his ideas with the rigorous analysis the consultant was accustomed to seeing. The second new director just didn't connect with the CEO on a personal level.

The two new directors formed an informal coalition and overpowered the rest of the board. At a dinner meeting during which they were to negotiate the CEO's upcoming contract, they sprang a surprise, telling him that his contract would not be renewed. Although the full board had not debated the issue, the CEO of course assumed they concurred. After the CEO's departure, the stock price and earnings plummeted, calling into question the judgment of those two dominant directors. The same two directors drove the selection of the new CEO, who had to be fired within a year. Those were costly mistakes that a better functioning board might not have made.

Without collegiality, a board can become paralyzed, but collegiality can go too far if it prevents directors from challenging a peer with a strong personality. That was the problem with one board, whose compensation committee chair used the force of his personality to push for his own view of what the CEO's targets should be. The CEO had delivered earnings per share of $1.30 and set a target of $1.60 for the coming year, which was above the industry growth rate and therefore represented a gain in market share. With no data or rationale to back his thinking, the comp committee chair determined that the CEO's target wasn't bold enough. He thought $1.70 was the right number.

The higher target posed a dilemma for the CEO. He was an aggressive leader who had sometimes exceeded his past targets, and the stock price had done well under his watch, but he knew he couldn't achieve the higher goal without making cuts that would haunt the company later. The target would be public, and compensation would be tied to it. If he missed, his credibility would be nicked, and the whole organization would feel deflated.

When the CEO met with the compensation committee, he tried to explain that doubling the industry growth rate in just one year was unrealistic, but the committee chair dominated the discussion, put the CEO on the defensive, and did not back off. The other committee members deferred to the chair. In the end, the CEO did meet the $1.70 target but only by cutting programs that were part of the company's longer-term growth plan. The consequences for the business would come to light three years later, after the CEO retired.

All these shortfalls in board effectiveness boil down to this: social dynamics. Boards need leaders who understand it and can shape it, so the board can exercise its collective judgment and do its job to the best of its collective ability. Given the pressures and sensitivities in today's corporate governance environment, it is crucial for boards to clearly outline the expectations and criteria for the role of the Lead Director, making social dynamics the centerpiece of it.

What a Lead Director Does

The most effective Lead Directors I've seen take their role very seriously, investing a lot of time and energy to build cohesiveness among board members and keep the group moving forward. They stay in close contact with directors and management and by their tone and response create an open line for directors and the CEO to voice concerns and make suggestions. Their receptiveness to diverse viewpoints and ability to convey information without the distortion of their own opinions builds trust.

They have their feelers out for issues that need to be surfaced and resolved and for any kind of "people problem" that is starting to brew. They have the skill to represent the board's view to management clearly and with an even hand, and they ask for management's views on how the board can help. They use their ground intelligence and sensitivity to social dynamics in three areas: to judge which issues are central to the board, to make board meetings more productive, and to enhance the relationship between management and the board.

Judging the Issues. It takes keen judgment to decide which issues need to be debated by the full board, which should be aired in executive session, and which require deft handling behind the scenes. Sometimes board members lock horns and can't reach consensus on an important issue. A skillful Lead Director can help the board move past it.

The board of one company faced a deadlock when directors were split on how the company should proceed during an industry consolidation. About half the board felt that because the industry was moving so fast, the company had to go on the offensive. Otherwise, it would become a target and lose control of its destiny. The rest of the board came down on the opposite side.

True, the industry was consolidating, but the company would have to take on a lot more debt to acquire other players, and it had a poor record of integrating new businesses. If it made acquisitions that it couldn't digest, the debt burden could be crushing. Unless the Lead Director remains impartial, these reservations and differences of opinion might not come out. A great Lead Director brings them into the open and helps the board sort through the pros and cons together.

A Lead Director is also a facilitator outside the boardroom. She might approach directors in private or at breaks to draw them out and see where they stand. She might get two directors talking over cocktails to better understand each other's thinking. She might then prompt them to give their views—and importantly, the facts behind them—in executive session, so all sides of the issue come into the open.

Creating transparency of opinions and the reasoning and data behind them gives the board a common foundation for discussing issues and makes it easier for the board to gel. The critical skill here is to articulate precisely and clearly the essence of issues that come before the board. The Lead Director's intellectual honesty in bringing forward both sides of an argument and focusing on the substance of the issues rather than the personalities driving them builds credibility and gains enormous respect.

Making Meetings More Productive. The Lead Director has an important role in board meetings, working in conjunction with the CEO to make them more productive. He can help the board focus on the most important issues in two ways: first, by working with the CEO to prioritize issues and set the agenda with the right allocation of time, and second, by making sure board discussions stay on track.

By staying in touch with all directors, the Lead Director knows what is on the board's mind. He can work with the CEO to hash out which topics are most important and figure out their sequencing and time allotment over the coming year.

Management will of course have items to bring to the board, but the board may want reports on areas management hasn't thought of, or with a wider lens or longer time horizon. As Andrea Jung, Avon CEO, says, "Board meetings present the opportunity to take a broader strategic look at the business and for the board and management to work together to anticipate the needs two years out." Items related directly to corporate governance, such as the board self-evaluation, must also be factored in.

The Lead Director also has a role to play in helping the CEO keep board discussions on track. In today's corporate governance environment, many CEOs are reluctant to push back at a director who makes a point repeatedly or vehemently for fear of seeming defensive. A Lead Director can intervene to make the dialogue more constructive.

Sometimes a CEO is unduly influenced by one dominant director, bending presentations toward the kinds of questions that director typically asks. The Lead Director should stay attuned to those dynamics and be prepared to use his interpersonal skills to keep the focus balanced.

At the same time, the Lead Director has to be willing to draw directors out. A board member might make a comment that's sharply worded or ask a question that seems offbeat, but the person might have a legitimate point. Without taking too much time out of the meeting, the Lead Director should help the director articulate it. One way to do this is to simply reframe the issue to bring the director's point to the surface: "Let me see if I got the right point here. Are you saying . . ." This gives the director a chance to clarify her thinking and communicate it more clearly.

Sometimes directors raise important issues, but the board and management are unprepared to take them on at that time, maybe because more background information or analysis is required. Then the challenge is to let the director be heard while postponing the discussion. Say the board is learning about the company's headway in an emerging market it is entering and where it will be making a major investment and transferring some technology. One director interjects: "Are the suppliers the right ones? Should you develop suppliers there at the same time?" The Lead Director might start by saying, "Interesting idea. Should we seek more information? What three questions should we ask management to answer next time?"

The Lead Director has to make judgments on the spot about what is simply too far off track to take the board's time. When it is, the Lead Director might step in, summarize the discussion, show how the point links to the discussion (if it does), and look toward the CEO and the director, suggesting, "That sounds like a good idea; maybe we should take it offline."

In one board meeting, a particular director told a senior executive who was presenting, "Make a note on the chart that you need to hire ten more people with special software skills." Then he got into a discussion on how to do outsourcing, cross-examining the presenter on some minute details not central to the main line of the discussion. The Lead Director gently intervened, "Those are issues for management to decide, not for us. We're pressed for time; maybe we can speed up a bit." Again, that's a comment better made by a Lead Director than a CEO.

When the Lead Director stays in close communication with the board, she will know when one director's opinion is an outlier that doesn't hold water. The Lead Director can solicit the board's help in countering it and bringing the discussion back to the center, saying, for example, "I think we also need to hear some other opinions on that." If a director is driving hard for his point of view, both the CEO and the Lead Director may have a hard time challenging him directly. But comments such as, "Let's think about some alternative approaches," or "What's another way to look at it?" provide an opening for management or another director to redirect the dialogue.

Building the CEO-Board Relationship. The Lead Director is a vital bridge between the CEO and the board. He or she is the one who gives the CEO feedback following executive sessions and sometimes provides coaching to the CEO. When the Lead Director speaks to a CEO after an executive session, he or she has to decide what feedback to give—and what not to give. The skill is partly in synthesizing what's said in the session: drawing out all viewpoints, judging the board's center of gravity, and reaching closure. It's also in the ability to communicate those points to the CEO in a straightforward way, with the right nuances.

Other board members are generally not present when the Lead Director speaks to the CEO, so the Lead Director has to have the utmost honesty and trustworthiness in conveying the board's thoughts, even when the feedback is tough. He might decide to present it in whatever way he thinks will help the CEO get it. But a CEO should never be surprised by performance issues because the Lead Director soft-pedaled on them. In one situation, when the CEO didn't get the bonus he thought he should, he nonetheless praised the Lead Director, saying, "You were very fair to me. You told me the board didn't think the pace was fast enough as things were evolving."

The same principle of candor and honesty holds true when reporting the CEO's response back to the board. If the accuracy is at all in question, another board member, for example, the governance committee chair, should accompany the Lead Director, and the CEO should respond to the full board directly.

Some tension in the board-management relationship is inherent, such as that between the CEO and the compensation committee. If it becomes overblown, however, the Lead Director might have to intervene. In these times, compensation committee chairs are in a particularly influential role. Their actions can have a huge impact on the CEO's relationship with the board. I have seen committee chairs take rigid positions because they were overly influenced by outside consultants or by their own personal experience or overly concerned about the optics of the committee's decisions to the outside world. Their stridency can adversely affect the CEO's attitude toward the chairman and strain communications between the two.

In such situations, the Lead Director is likely to know about the tension between the comp committee chair and the CEO. He might step in to facilitate communication or become a mediator between the two, or he might even encourage them to bring the issue to the executive session.

The Lead Director is a sounding board for the CEO and may be in the best position to see when the chief executive could benefit from some coaching in a particular area. With the backing of the full board, the Lead Director himself might provide that coaching or help identify another director or an outsider to play that role.

How to Choose a Lead Director

Appointing a Lead Director is becoming a political process in many cases because of the prestige associated with it. Directors do campaign for leadership positions such as Lead Director or the chairs of committees as if they were running for office—a subtle process that itself can erode the board's group dynamic. (To be sure, no one campaigns to be audit committee chair.)

Choosing a Lead Director is not a referendum on who's the smartest or who has the longest tenure. The selection must be based on who has the right social skills, incisiveness, and personality traits. He or she must also have the temperament and time for the job, and take the assignment very seriously. A candidate should anticipate the time requirements and honestly weigh whether they will be able to devote the time as well as the emotional energy it takes to be a Lead Director. In the fall of 2008, I gained great admiration for a few Lead Directors who were unflappable in a time of crisis. Their dedication and temperaments had a calming effect at a time when it really mattered. A Lead Director needs superb *social skills*. She must be good at detecting subtle cues and articulate in communicating without distortion or unwanted nuance. She must be able to draw directors out, encouraging them to probe the issues and express their views, while gently steering them away from blind alleys and minutiae. She must also be able to guide and sometimes counsel fellow directors or the CEO. A Lead Director can do none of that without trust and good chemistry with other directors and the CEO.

Furthermore, the person must have *keen business judgment and incisiveness*. She must have the ability to sense what is really on the board's mind and, by making judgments on whether an issue needs to be explored more fully or is peripheral, help the board focus on the right things.

Not all issues are well articulated. A good Lead Director has exceptional instincts to sense when an important question is emerging and bring it forward. At one company, a very successful CEO made a mega acquisition about a year before he planned to retire. As his successor was still settling into the new job, global economic conditions changed dramatically, drastically reducing commodities prices and upending the situation envisioned at the time the mega acquisition was made.

Several directors saw that the emerging conditions would sharply erode the value of the asset they had just acquired and that shareholder value would thus decline. The company might even have to take a write-down, affecting the company's ratings. They began to think the company should reverse its decision and divest as soon as possible, but they weren't sure others would see it the same way. That kind of uncertainty often prevents directors from raising issues in a formal setting, but a savvy Lead Director listens for them and doesn't let them slide by.

During cocktails, one of those directors might say to the Lead Director, "I see recession coming in, and it could cut the price of that asset in half. I wonder if we need to shed the acquisition. What do you think?" The Lead Director might respond, "That's an important issue. Why don't you talk to the CEO about it? I think he'll be receptive to it." Or the Lead Director might suggest taking up the issue in executive session and, if the board doesn't subscribe to their fellow director's point of view, could suggest defining some early warning signals to jointly watch.

Directors cannot easily change their *personality traits*. A Lead Director needs the right ones: composure, an even temperament, courage, and containment of his ego. When others get impassioned or downright stubborn, the Lead Director must be a calming influence and at times the voice of reason.

A great Lead Director explores and invites diverse viewpoints yet has the courage to do what is needed to make the board function better. He has the confidence to subtly intervene to redirect the discussion or to shut down a line of nitpicky questioning with no formal authority to do so.

The most critical personality trait, though, is to not let ego get out of hand. When one CEO proposed a strategic acquisition in a foreign country with highly volatile political and economic conditions, it sparked a flurry of debate in the strategy session. The acquisition would give the company a platform for building market share, but the company itself was in a turnaround and management had a lot on its plate. The target company was owned by three families, and it wasn't clear that they would give up 100 percent of their ownership, although they would likely give up a minority stake.

Based on his experience of having gone through similar situations twice, the Lead Director had a distinct view of the present situation. "Why don't we acquire 51% of the company and structure a buyout of the remaining shares in three phases over three years?" he suggested. "That way, we can keep management on board and the family-owners can maintain a share of earnings over several years."

A second director then asked, "Can I give you a counterpoint?"

"Absolutely," replied the Lead Director in an open and inviting tone. "I encourage it."

"I've gone through three acquisitions along those lines, so let me describe my perspective. If the buyout flourishes, that's great; your plan will work out fine. But if it doesn't, and if there are any roadblocks along the way, you're going to have to manage some unhappy minority shareholders. How will you divide the earnings at that point? How do you resolve who owns the financing? It's a slim chance, but if it went down that road, there could be some bad blood. We might even end up in arbitration and litigation. Is that a risk we want to take?"

Other directors and the CEO got engaged in the debate, and together they identified what further questions management needed to ask and what additional data was needed. The board also encouraged management to think about how to keep its foot in the door if it was decided that the acquisition didn't make sense at that time. The point is that the debate was enriched because the Lead Director welcomed viewpoints that differed from his own and engaged the board without automatically deferring to or opposing management.

A contained ego can also make peer review more effective. It sometimes falls to the Lead Director to deliver the feedback to the individual directors. In doing so, the Lead Director must be clear that he is representing the board as a whole and not pitting his own perception against that director. That makes the feedback more palatable and preserves the objectivity and trust the Lead Director needs to carry out the role. For a Lead Director to make a significant contribution, it's important that she occupy this leadership position for more than one year. A typical tenure today is three years. Some companies rotate the Lead Director position annually, but it might take a while for the Lead Director to build rapport, and it's disruptive to recreate the board dynamics every year. By the same token, there must be safeguards against someone becoming a super director who wields too much individual power. A term of three years for a Lead Director seems about right.

How CEOs Affect Board Dynamics

CEOs have a tremendous opportunity to shape board dynamics through their formal and informal communications with the board, committees, and individual directors. What the CEO chooses as agenda items, how he or she conducts board meetings, the tone of responses to questions and requests, and his or her receptiveness to feedback all make the CEO-board relationship better or worse. Getting to the heart of the issues quickly makes a difference, because whatever is presented first to the board has an outsized influence on the board dynamics of the meeting to follow.

Focusing on the issues rather than personalities helps defuse conflicts. Inviting feedback and allowing time for it demonstrate that the CEO is receptive to the board's ideas. It's natural for the CEO to seek input from certain directors more than others depending on the issue at hand and for some directors to communicate more frequently with the CEO, but the CEO must keep in mind the need for transparency. Speaking to only some directors between board meetings can create a two-tier board and lead to power struggles between competing factions. CEOs can avoid those problems by building relationships with all directors and keeping the lines of communication open.

Key Points

- Leadership, usually from the Lead Director, plays a big role in creating the positive social dynamic that a board's effectiveness depends upon.
- An effective Lead Director is one who can zero in on key issues, make meetings more productive by keeping dialogue on track, and strengthen the relationship between the CEO and the board.

- A good business leader doesn't necessarily make for a good Lead Director. The Lead Director's real job requirements are social skills and a special blend of temperament and personality.

- Boards should outline what their Lead Director will do, and have a clear process for assigning the role based on the requirements of the job.

Question 9.

IS OUR GOVERNANCE COMMITTEE BEST OF BREED?

Governance committees have a newfound importance: it's their job to ensure that the board is an effective boss to the CEO. That means ensuring that the board has the people, processes, and leadership it needs to leverage its intellectual clout on behalf of the business. It also means correcting whatever stands in the way of good governance. Whether the obstacle is dysfunctional board dynamics, a toxic relationship between the board and management, or lack of necessary expertise on the board, the governance committee must be prepared to take it on. All of this may seem like a tall order, but in today's world, no governance committee can consider itself world class unless it defines its role clearly and broadly, and takes appropriate actions in a timely manner.

Governance committees must raise their game, just as audit committees have done in the wake of Sarbanes-Oxley. They must take ownership for the board's *output*. Is the board in fact making a contribution? What changes must the board make to improve its contributions—its output—and get a better return on its time? Leaders of the board—the board chair, Lead Director, and committee chairs—have important roles to play in helping the board work effectively, but good governance cannot fall on the shoulders of a few individuals. That's why the governance committee is pivotal.

There are several different dimensions to the committee's role. These include defining the board's leadership roles and setting the policies for selecting board leaders and transitioning directors off the board, assessing the committee structure and making committee assignments, and carrying out processes to continuously improve the board and keep it evergreen. In doing all that, the committee must be attuned to the human factors as well as the mechanics of board processes, because poor individual behavior and lousy board dynamics can bring good governance to a screeching halt.

Ensure Appropriate Board Leadership

A leaderless group is bound to fail. Boards have their leaders—the chair, Lead Director, and committee chairs—and they have tremendous influence on how the board functions, for better or worse. A good leader helps the group deepen its discussion and find consensus; a poor leader lets the group splinter or wander, or worse, uses his position for personal power. The governance committee must recognize the importance of those positions and create rules for assigning them that reduce the risk of politicking and power plays.

The governance committee should define the roles and criteria for different positions, and think through the length of the terms, keeping in mind the need to make optimal use of directors' talents while keeping the board dynamics in balance. It's important to select leaders with a keen sensitivity to their skills in getting the best out of the board, and thereby improving the board's ability to govern. When it comes to appointing a Lead Director, there is one nonnegotiable the committee can't afford to miss: the person must have the *social skills* needed to carry out the job.

The Lead Director is a special position that not everybody is suited for. In fact, some boards might find they need to recruit a director specifically to fill that role. I have seen great Lead Directors—like Jack Krol, named Director of the Year by the National Association of Corporate Director in 1998—do a spectacular job of knitting the board and management, and others who incorrectly believed the position entitled them to a stronger voice than their fellow board members. A crisp definition of the Lead Director role can stem misunderstandings about what the position entails. And rotating the job every three years seems about right for creating continuity while preventing a hold on power.

A lot of board work gets done in committees, so committee chairs can make a huge difference to the board's output. The governance committee needs to be deliberate in making those assignments. Not every member of a committee has the qualities to lead the group, even if they make great contributions to the committee and are effective leaders in other parts of their lives. In assigning committee chairs, the governance committee should take into account the person's expertise as well as her ability to lead the group. Rotating those positions is a good idea, but some committee chairs require special expertise and are very time consuming. That's a practical reality the board has to deal with and that might have implications for recruiting future board members.

The governance committee will have to select its own leadership and should set some rules for making that decision. Chair of the governance committee is often seen as a prestigious position, and there can be political jockeying for it. To avoid such awkwardness, the criteria for the chair should be explicit. Keep in mind that it's a sensitive position, because that person often has to deal with human behavior that could adversely affect the functioning of the board. The chair may have to confront a director whose behavior is disruptive, and is usually the one to convey the results of a peer review. It is a truism that in any social group some members will be less effective than others and some are potentially unacceptable.

The individual must therefore be highly trusted by directors and management alike—an "elder statesman" type, with great instincts in dealing with people. Of course, that person must be able to commit the time required as well. Because of the need to develop rapport, it may be wise to appoint governance committee chairs for longer terms, perhaps three to four years. But at some point, the position should rotate.

Use Committees Wisely—But Don't Isolate Them

All public boards have audit, compensation, and nominating or governance committees. Most add other committees as they are needed, for strategy/innovation, risk, marketing, supply chain, technology, or social responsibility, for example. What work needs to be done in committee? How will the committee interface with the board and with management? Those are questions the governance committee needs to work out in collaboration with management and the board. Each committee needs to have a clear written charter and its own twelve-month priorities.

Committees must be extensions of the board, not replacements for it. In the past, committees went off on their own and came back to the board with recommendations that were invariably rubber-stamped. That approach is out of date. In today's environment, directors are uncomfortable signing off on issues they don't fully understand, and besides, committees don't always have the full range of perspectives.

Committees therefore should tap the intellectual horsepower and expertise of the full board, even as they take command of their area. One approach I've seen several boards use to great benefit is for the committee chairs to stay in communication with directors who are not committee members. By simply picking up the phone, the chair can test out the committee's ideas and get input from other appropriate board members. The committee still does all the legwork, holding meetings and conference calls, working with management, and talking to outside advisors such as auditors and compensation consultants. There's no way the full board can take the time to do all that. But there are always issues that arise along the way, on which other directors' opinions could be useful.

In recommending the performance targets for management in a period of great economic uncertainty and deciding whether they should be based on a point estimate or a range, a compensation committee might, for instance, seek the views of fellow directors who are dealing with those issues in their own companies or are especially attuned to the realities of the external landscape, including public opinion. One compensation committee tapped the strategy expertise of a non-committee member in order to help refine some of the CEO's compensation metrics. That director didn't need to weigh in on all the committee's deliberations, but he was still able to help specify which metrics would reflect management's progress in implementing the strategy in the evolving recessionary environment.

The committee chair should decide whom to reach out to and when, and bring that information back to the committee as they formulate their recommendations. On some critical issues, such as CEO succession, the committee can't assume its recommendation will be accepted as is. The full board needs to vet it. And it's the governance committee that should make sure that time in board meetings is appropriately allocated.

Committee membership should rotate every few years. I'm not suggesting a strict rotation where everyone moves one chair to the right. That wouldn't make sense, since some directors are clearly suited for particular committees—accounting backgrounds for audit committees, HR backgrounds for compensation committees, and so on. But serving on different committees broadens directors' knowledge. It also contains any concentration of power that might emerge among a clique of directors. I recommend a switch every three to four years, for committees and chairs, including the governance committee.

Ensure the Board Functions Well

For a governance committee to be world class, it must be assertive when it needs to be, and find ways to deal with the highly sensitive but very real human problems that prevent the board from doing its job well. It helps if the governance committee consists of at least three to five people. As a committee, they will be able to talk through and cross-check one another's perceptions of the board dynamics. One issue that can be hard to pinpoint is when centers of power are starting to form on the board. Cliques form naturally among groups of people, but boards shouldn't allow a small handful of directors to become the de facto interface with the CEO or the decision driver, while the others struggle for airtime. They need to ensure all key issues get to the board as a whole.

When the working relationship between the board and the CEO begins to erode, the governance committee should probe why that might be happening. Is it a communications issue that the Lead Director and CEO can work on together to resolve? Is there an information gap on the part of some directors—for example, are some board members not up-to-speed on strategy? The committee should be prepared to resolve those issues.

The governance committee should also protect the line between managing and governing. When a director starts micromanaging in the midst of a discussion, the Lead Director may be able to handle the problem on the spot. But if the problem is recurring, the governance committee should prompt the Lead Director to go further. Speaking with the director privately, with a respectful and constructive tone, often cures the problem. The majority of directors are quite responsive when they learn they are detracting from the group. If, however, the Lead Director has trouble handling the issue for whatever reason, the governance committee should raise it in committee and incorporate it in the board's peer evaluation.

The governance committee should do one more thing to ensure the board functions well: administer a board self-evaluation. A well-designed evaluation is a great resource for spotting problems in how the board is functioning. Management's opinion is important; the governance committee should reach out to the CEO to uncover how much management values the board's input. I am also a strong advocate of doing a peer review, because it gives directors a confidential outlet for concerns about individual behavior that may be a drag on board effectiveness. That could just mean encouraging a respected colleague to speak more. The governance committee should ensure that the evaluation is robust and that the board translates the findings into specific action plans and follows through on them, whether it's searching for a director with particular domain expertise, changing how management reports to the board, forming a new committee, or asking an existing director to move on.

Driving for Continuous Improvement and Self-Renewal

Helping the board become better at its job doesn't have to be a once-a-year activity coinciding with an annual self-evaluation. The governance committee should actively seek best practices in corporate governance through well-established educational programs, professional organizations, and personal networks. Part of that drive for continuous improvement will entail keeping the board's composition up-to-date.

Devising a long-term board succession process is a central task of the governance committee. That means identifying the expertise the board will need on an ongoing basis, what candidates will fill those roles and how to vet them, when transitions might need to be made, and how to execute those transitions.

One company's governance committee was alert to those needs when a director passed away. The CEO gravitated toward adding someone with CFO experience, because the former director had been a CFO. But the governance committee realized that what the board would miss most was the deceased director's deep supply chain knowledge. That knowledge was of increasing importance because of the company's heavy dependence on overseas sourcing. The board recruited a Hong Kong–based logistics chief instead of a CFO, and the CEO couldn't be happier.

Boards shouldn't wait for natural transitions, like mandatory retirements or a director's untimely demise. Moving people off a board can be sensitive but is sometimes necessary. Governance committees need to have a director resignation policy—both for voluntary and involuntary transitions. Mandatory retirement ages or term limits are one way to ease voluntary transitions. And sometimes, great directors recognize when they should step aside to make room for fresh blood. The more clarity the governance committee creates around transitions, the easier it is for a director to step down on his or her own.

Still, many boards will face awkward involuntary transitions. I remember one governance committee with three members who got riled up when talking about the micromanaging of a fellow director. The problem had become so chronic, they had no choice but to denominate him from the board. "We've got to get rid of that pontificator," one governance committee member said, in the heat of the moment. Fortunately, they first spoke with the Lead Director and with committee chairs, and they were very polite and diplomatic when they recommended to the offending director that he not stand for re-nomination. The director left without incident, and they brought on a new director who had deep knowledge of branding and worked well with the rest of the board. Every board will need to make a transition at some point; it falls to the governance committee to actively manage the process.

The Problem of Unwanted Directors

Many boards have a director or two who render the collective body ineffective or create unwarranted strain in the CEO-board relationship. Boards must face the problem and deal with it. Allowing the problem to continue can have a devastating effect when emergency situations arise. The following behaviors, reported by directors about their peers, are tell-tale signs that the director is unwanted.

- "The director pontificates and adds no value. It wastes a lot of our time."
- "He is out of touch with contemporary happenings. Maybe he's been retired too long."
- "She has too much to do. She can't give the board enough time."
- "He repeats the same objection over and over again, even when it doesn't really matter or the board has already decided against it."
- "There's a personal animosity between the director and the CEO. He always puts the CEO on the defensive."
- "Her questions are too narrow and at too low a level. She's no longer respected."
- "He's jockeying for a job in the company, as CEO or COO."
- "She's always pushing the CEO to use advisors she's used in the past. When he doesn't, she holds it against him."
- "He gets sidetracked on his Blackberry, then suddenly interrupts the flow of the discussion. We're tired of it."
- "She takes a lot of air time, and sours the mood for the rest of the meeting."
- "He is getting senile. He actually falls asleep in the meetings."

Boards must come to terms with the fact that no process of selecting directors is perfect and that times change. Governance committees must ensure that their boards have a process in place to move unwanted directors out.

Key Points

- The governance committee has a pivotal role in ensuring the board functions well enough to own up to its responsibilities. It should define its role broadly and be assertive in holding the board to a high standard.

- The governance committee must think through the criteria for various board leadership roles, balancing expertise with sensitivity to human behavior, and rotate committee assignments and chairs to avoid pockets of power.

- The governance committee is responsible for turning around faltering board dynamics.

- The governance committee must be sensitive to the CEO-board relationship, and pay attention to how well the board is respected by management.

- The governance committee must take charge of board succession, including identifying and vetting director candidates, and making sure transitions off the board are handled in a timely and appropriate manner.

Question 10.

HOW DO WE GET THE MOST VALUE OUT OF OUR LIMITED TIME?

It's undeniable that the demands on directors' time are rising, and that fact has become an unrelenting source of frustration for many directors. "We only meet six times a year, and we don't get paid a whole lot," one director complained at a recent board gathering. "A lot is expected of us."

First things first: deal with it. Complaints like that coming from the captains of industry are inappropriate. The days of holding a half-day meeting every other month have passed. Boards need to commit the time that's really needed to do the job—full-day board meetings, committee calls and meetings as frequently as needed, and lots of preparation time outside the boardroom. Your bosses—the company's owners—deserve better. Their expectations for directors are higher for good reason, and the watchdogs are watching carefully. In the fall of 2008, the boards of several major companies held four or more meetings over the course of eight weeks. All members of the board had to change their schedules on short notice. But they all made the commitment to attend every meeting.

By the same token, boards need to get more value out of the time directors spend together. Many feel the problem isn't just the number of hours; it's the return they are getting on that time. In some cases, boards feel too much time is spent on routine items and resolutions, and not enough on the issues that have a significant impact on the business—things like strategy, risk, and succession. Just when the discussion gets interesting, some directors excuse themselves to catch their flights, even though they would like to stay. In other cases, directors feel helpless when a colleague goes off on a tangent, draining precious meeting time and psychological energy. Management also loses time when they feel compelled to respond to directors' every request, even the trivial ones.

It's easy to see how board meetings can get bogged down into reviews of quarterly financial numbers, particularly given the accounting issues that damaged so many companies in the recent past. But boards and management teams can take simple steps to make more efficient use of their time. Indeed, a valuable use of time is to discuss in executive session how the board can set its priorities, run board meetings, and improve communications to ensure that it not only monitors the company's financials but also preserves time to make even higher-level contributions. Boards and CEOs need to work together to improve the return on their time.

How Can the Board Stay Focused on Its Priorities?

Boards don't make five million decisions over the course of the year; there are usually only a handful of issues and decisions that significantly impact the business. Making them explicit helps the board focus on them. The CEO and the board's leadership should identify those four or five, at most six, items that should constitute the bulk of the board's time and energy in the coming year. They should state them in a *twelve-month priorities list* and clarify when they should be revisited in the boardroom, for how long, and what interim steps are needed.

At one company in fall 2008, for example, the board discussed six items to include on the twelve-month priorities list, after completing a review of the strategy:

1. Stress test liquidity and the possibility of violating debt covenants under the high probability of deep recession and

restricted credit availability (a top priority because this company is highly leveraged).

2. Have management prepare and present a new plan for the allocation of capital should cash flow decline materially. Monitor a quarterly dashboard of cash flow and other measures of liquidity.

3. Discuss in depth the opportunities for acquisitions under evolving conditions of recession and changes in the capital markets.

4. Discuss in depth the plan to more aggressively move into China despite slowing growth. Explore what the company could do for the long term.

5. Discuss which of the three players in the succession line appears to be developing in ways that are better suited to the evolving external conditions.

6. Discuss management's plan B to address changing conditions.

The board of a company in a turnaround might want to make cash and operational benchmarks a top priority. The board of a company in a consolidating industry might want to carve out time for updates on mergers and acquisitions, how the competitive landscape is changing, and the viability of its own strategy. Every board should consider for its twelve-month priorities some kind of *strategic* dashboard, a set of measures that go beyond the typical operational and financial metrics to link with the company's long-term value. And following an acquisition, the board should make follow-up on post-merger integration a boardroom priority.

A list of clear, explicit priorities not only helps the board focus on the big picture but also aligns management and the board and provides continuity from meeting to meeting. The board should be reminded of the twelve-month priorities in every meeting, whether by the CEO, Lead Director, or nonexecutive chair. Or the list can be at the front of the board briefing packet sent to all directors.

That doesn't mean every priority is discussed in every board meeting. Some will require research from the management team so the board can have an informed discussion at a later date. The board may even need to commission, through management, analysis from outside sources. And of course, as emergencies erupt or new issues arise, the board has to adjust its priorities.

How Can We Design Board Meetings to Run More Efficiently?

A typical board meeting begins with a review of financials and housekeeping resolutions. Obviously, directors need to deal with them, but some of these peripheral issues chew up the bulk of the board's meeting time. That's because people tend to react to whatever is presented first, even if the intention was to just "get them out of the way."

One CEO told me he lost a third of his presentation time when he gave what he intended to be a brief follow-up report on negotiations with a CFO candidate the board had previously approved. He wanted to tell the board that the negotiations were proceeding within the guidelines the board had provided, and then move quickly to higher-priority issues. But one director kept digging for more detail on the negotiating positions, and the CEO felt obliged to respond. The board lost thirty minutes of its four-hour meeting time and the group's whole mood and energy level flagged.

That's why I suggest that the most important issues on the agenda come first. One financial services firm moved the meaty items to the top of the agenda, renaming the remainder the "consent agenda." It made a huge difference in improving the board's return on its time. The directors keep an eye on the clock to make sure there's enough time for the resolutions on the consent agenda, of course. But they don't use the psychology of getting minor things out of the way first. Some chairs and presiding directors are skillful at managing time. As they get closure on an issue, they remind the group how much time is left. After a while, the group gets used to the rhythm of the meeting.

Distilling at the end of the meeting the issues that came up is a good way to refocus the board on its priorities going forward. At the end of board meetings at Austin Industries, on whose board I serve, the CEO articulates the most critical things he heard and needs to act on. He distills the discussion on the spot, articulating the takeaways. The purpose of the distillation is for the CEO to test the items he perceives to be at the center of the whole board's deliberations, and that require follow through. The board can validate that the CEO has covered all the important bases. (Alternatively, the Lead Director or another board member can do the distillation.)

As time demands increase and boards become more watchful of how they use their face-to-face meeting time, they should take care not to squeeze out *unstructured time* together. Social time allows directors to get to know each other better and builds trust. It's an important building block of a board's group dynamics. Besides, many a useful insight have emerged from casual conversation at dinner following an all-day board meeting. Equally important are informal dinners, usually prior to board meetings, with high-potential leaders. These gatherings help directors get to know the leadership team, assess and mentor the team, and improve the leadership pipeline and succession processes. It is time well spent.

How Can Management's Reports Improve Boardroom Dialogue?

Most of the information packages management sends out before board meetings are chock full of great data, but the directions on what to do with it are usually dismal. Presenting page after page of data is almost begging directors to nit-pick. Management can raise the "altitude" of boardroom discussion by telling the board upfront what issues to focus on and what the salient questions are, in order of importance.

Presenting cogent analysis in a two- to four-page document gives directors an incisive overview of the upcoming meeting. If the relevant information is scattered in multiple exhibits, create a new one so directors can see the relationships among those pieces, and with that, state a conclusion. A call-out might read, for example, "You can see that we are winning against the competition by a hundred basis points in market share. The reason is we had an exciting marketing campaign last quarter."

When presenting the data, don't merely repeat it. A typical presenter might drone on, "My sales went up from $100 million to $110 million." The directors have already read that. Help them understand the cause: "The increase in sales was because of the launch of three products. And, going forward, we expect sales to go from $110 to $130, largely because we just entered a new geography." Then invite the directors to discuss the drivers and risks of growth. Their questions will undoubtedly be at a higher level and add more value: What competitive reaction are you anticipating? What could the company do to expand more quickly? What resources will be needed? Are there issues we should know about regarding suppliers, given the time delay of imports from China?

In the summer of 2008, a prominent beverage company saw its sales decline rather precipitously. At around the same time, bottlers had increased the price of the beverage by about 3 percent. The company did some consumer research and found that the number of bottles and cans consumed per person per day had slipped. Further research found that consumers were holding onto their drinks longer, and the decline in demand was attributable to that change in consumer behavior. That kind of analysis lays the foundation for the board to ask provocative and important questions, such as: What's causing the behavior to change? What ideas do you have to increase consumption versus to gain market share? How long is this consumption decline going to last?

The same principles should apply to all presentations made to the board, including those made by a CEO's direct reports.

CEOs have a tendency to delegate to the presenter; they should more actively coach their subordinates to structure information and lead discussion in a way that makes the most of the board-room time. Most CEOs are directors elsewhere so they should know what a good information architecture looks like and how sequencing affects the quality of the dialogue. They should enlist the help of their CFO and one or two directors to get the architecture of the information right.

If a presentation is structured and presented well, it will leave plenty of time for discussion. One director shared a simple idea for CEOs to facilitate dialogue: "Just tell us clearly what the issue is, the context, the alternatives you've thought through, your view of which way to go, and what you'd like from the board. That's it. For most presentations, you can do it in five or six slides, including supporting data." On many issues, management should plan for discussion time equal to the presentation time. Presenters should understand that their time is short and that they are not expected to address every possible question. Their job is to create a foundation for the board to have an informed discussion and to respond to whatever questions arise.

How Much Time Should We Commit?

There's no benchmark that determines how much time a director should be engaged with the board in a given year, because at the end of the day, a board will be measured by its output—the value it adds—not by the hours spent getting there. Still, it's clear that to make any substantive contribution to a public company board, a four-hour board meeting won't be enough. Six board meetings a year seems to be enough if the meetings are almost a full day with another half day reserved for committee meetings—and of course assuming a focused agenda and dialogue. At Tyco Electronics (one of the boards I serve on), despite having a half dozen meet-ings a year, we don't find ourselves pressed for time. We almost always finish the board meeting on time or even a few minutes early, having covered substantive issues in depth. The way the board receives information, choice of topics, and leadership of the meetings are all contributing factors. We get a high return on our time because the board functions so well.

All companies send briefings out to directors before meetings. It's a director's responsibility to review them thoroughly and come to board meetings prepared to discuss them. Likewise, directors have to be prepared to spend quality time in committees, where the smaller size of the group can more efficiently process in-depth discussions, either in person or by conference call. And just because something is delegated to a committee doesn't mean non-committee members are off the hook. The objective is to tap the intellectual power of the full board without infringing on the board's face-to-face time. Committee chairs should stay in touch with non-committee members to gather input from them when appropriate. And the full board needs to fully vet the committees' recommendations, without nit-picking.

All of these tasks require time and dedication, which every director must be willing to devote. Society will demand it.

How Can Directors Fill Knowledge Gaps More Efficiently?

It's not unusual for directors to have gaps in their understanding of the company's strategy, industry, money-making, or external conditions that can create opportunities or extreme stress. Directors all have their own expertise and interests. Some are good at the operating details, while others understand the customer side of things. Some have a good fix on geopolitics, while others are great on the internals. Only a few understand the anatomy of enterprise risk, and each may have a different understanding of the company's strategy.

One way to fill these gaps and keep directors informed and up-to-date without taking boardroom time is to arrange tutorial sessions for them. I have seen this practice work well: a small group of two or three directors at a time sits down with the CEO and his or her operating team in an informal setting on whatever topic is appropriate, whether it's the mechanics of revenue recognition or an overview of the essentials of the business. There might be a brief presentation, but it is mostly a Q&A facilitated by the CEO. Questions can drill down to a lower altitude than boardroom discussions allow, say, into specific issues around recession. There should be an informal air, so directors feel comfortable asking virtually any question.

These tutorials are not just for new directors or those who have limited business experience. Even long-time directors occasionally need a refresher on some aspect of the business. And it doesn't matter how expert a director is in his or her own business; every business is unique. Besides, some directors love digging into areas they know a lot about or just happen to be interested in. This way, they can satisfy their curiosity and do their due diligence without taking the whole board down a rabbit hole. Meeting time is cleared for the big issues in which every board member must be fully engaged.

Key Points

- Directors should work with the CEO to improve the "return on their time." If more time is needed, directors should devote it without complaint.

- Boards should define their priorities and preserve meeting time to discuss them.

- Management can raise the altitude of discussions by giving directors a brief, cogent analysis before the meeting. The two- to four-page document should state the causes for company performance and point directors toward issues and questions they need to address.

Question 11.

HOW CAN EXECUTIVE SESSIONS HELP THE BOARD OWN UP?

The executive session is the single most important innovation in corporate governance to date. It balances the power between the CEO and the board. No matter how dominant a CEO is, the fact that he or she is not in the room when the board meets speaks volumes. It also eliminates the need for clandestine talk among directors. And it can help the group of independent directors gel.

When executive sessions first came into use, they sometimes caused strain in the relationship between CEOs and their boards. Even now, if executive sessions are not run well, they can undermine trust and clog the flow of information and ideas, which makes it harder for the board to do its job. Sometimes strain is unavoidable, particularly when the company is not performing well. But under normal circumstances, executive sessions should enhance the CEO-board relationship by allowing the board's faintest concerns to surface sooner, when there is still time for the CEO to address them. At the same time, it's a great opportunity for directors to share with the CEO what's on their minds.

The whole point of executive sessions is informality. Having all the independent directors together without the CEO changes the social ambiance of the group and lowers barriers. But that's not to say they can become free-for-alls. It takes skill to conduct the sessions in a way that makes directors comfortable speaking their mind candidly. When the tone is right, the board chemistry evolves, and directors don't hesitate to raise the *real* issues. Putting them on the table for constructive discussion later with the CEO builds mutual understanding and strengthens the bridge between management and the board. The relationship can and does get better.

What Should—and Shouldn't—We Talk About in the Executive Session?

Executive sessions are a great forum to get outside directors talking in a different way about critical issues from strategy, execution, and performance to the company's leaders, general macroeconomic conditions, and the functioning of the board itself. In fact, the board's self-evaluation should be discussed in the executive session every year.

Directors can ask questions that might have sounded naïve with the chief executive present; they can air their thoughts, float trial balloons, or test counterpoints and brainstorm or cross-check them together without that awkward feeling that they might be embarrassing themselves or the CEO. They can voice ideas or thoughts that occur to them outside the board meeting, when they've had a chance to sit back and reflect on things.

In one executive session, the Lead Director noted that the strategy presentation made earlier that day was excellent and the discussion had been very rich. He was impressed with the management team that developed the strategy. Other board members chimed in, saying that the operational changes needed to support the strategy were well thought through.

As the chit-chat continued, one director, who unlike many other directors had no operational background, wondered aloud, "Do you think the three-year goal presented in the strategy is bold enough to excite investors? Frankly, it doesn't excite me."

The CEO had proposed a goal of 4 percent growth for 2008, which was in line with the growth of the industry. But the total market was huge. "Shouldn't we be thinking about double-digit growth in the longer-term?" the director continued. "Our best competitor is getting 7 percent, and its price-earnings ratio is significantly higher. We should explore what some of the trends are that we could tap into."

As every director knows, the flow of conversation among such sharp-minded people can turn very quickly. Within ten minutes, the directors came around to decide the target was too low. Even the Lead Director, who was initially so effusive, recalibrated his thoughts.

The director who challenged the goals probably wouldn't have done so in a regular board meeting, especially when his peers supported them so enthusiastically and were ready to move on. But the ambiance of the executive session allowed the issue to surface. The Lead Director then took it on himself to talk to the CEO about the board's thinking, suggesting he think about bolder goals and engage the board in different options during the year. The Lead Director was clear and respectful to the CEO, and the CEO was neither confused nor demoralized.

At another company, the board had been gradually getting to know two CEO succession candidates, one of whom was a clear front-runner to replace the retiring CEO two years out. In the executive session, directors commented on a division head, not on the succession list, who had caught their attention. In an earlier presentation, this leader had had ambitious goals for diversifying and growing his business—too ambitious, the board thought at the time. But the division head fulfilled his promises. His strategy for the business was right, and he pulled it off masterfully.

As the directors talked, they concurred that this division head was a great strategic thinker, even more so than the current CEO. Although the person had not been identified as a contender for the CEO job, the board began to discuss his potential. There was overall agreement that he might well be the next CEO, and they agreed to suggest that the CEO put him in a broader job soon to test him.

In other cases, executive sessions have led to recommendations for the CEO to hire a COO, or to commission research from investment banks or strategy firms. The board may even decide to consult advisors on its own, particularly in cases when it needs counsel on legal or ethical issues.

Directors should have freedom to raise hunches and ask questions about almost any topic under the board's purview. But there are some things to avoid. I've seen some executive sessions devolve into a review of the presentation: "That slide was wrong," or "Why did that presentation take so long?" That kind of feedback can be provided to the CEO directly; it doesn't need to take time from the group. The executive session can quickly get eaten up by discussions of minutiae.

Discussing the overall focus or quality of management presentations is a different story. In one executive session, a director noted that the presentations by division heads seemed like budgeting exercises. "We need to see the bigger picture," he noted. "We should be talking about emerging trends and competitive reactions, with a longer-term view." The board agreed, and the Lead Director passed the feedback to the CEO, who worked with his team. Two months later when the next division head came before the board, the presentation was indeed more strategic, and the board got mentally engaged, asking incisive questions and making a real intellectual contribution in less than the three hours allotted. When a discussion finishes ahead of the appointed time and there are no more questions left to explore after a spirited and energized discussion, it generates a feeling of deep satisfaction among directors and management.

Set the Right Tone for Executive Sessions

Getting directors to open up sometimes requires skill. The person leading the executive session (usually the Lead Director or the nonexecutive chair) can ask some very broad questions to break the ice, such as, How do we feel about how things are going? The purpose of informality is to make sure the psychological barriers are low so all voices will be heard.

Any and every director should be able to ask questions, respond to peers, and raise issues he or she is not sure about. The Lead Director should draw out directors who seem reticent, zero in on key points, and not let the conversation wander too far. He or she must also make sure the points are based in fact and there is some rigor to them. No shallow thinking allowed. Keeping the group open but within bounds requires skill, and boards would do well to select a Lead Director specifically with that ability in mind.

Sometimes controversial issues are brewing beneath the surface. The executive session is the place to discuss them. If nobody mentions them, perhaps out of politeness, the Lead Director may need to step up and raise the issue. He or she should push for discussion and let the pros and cons come out, so the issue doesn't linger.

To be sure, executive sessions are a great venue to test concerns about the company's senior leaders and discuss them. But directors should focus on substance and be careful about their wording. The Lead Director should be particularly sensitive to directors who are not thoughtful in their criticism of the CEO or members of the team. By that I mean directors should avoid criticism that doesn't lead to anything. In one executive session, a director thought the CEO was being defensive, and said so. The CEO courteously said he didn't think he was. The director held to his view: "Yes you are." The tone of the director's remark was not conducive to good discussion and caught the rest of the board by surprise. The Lead Director did not intervene. Everyone in the room could sense the strain in the social atmosphere.

Directors should find ways to push back on the issue rather than at the CEO as a person. With the exception of turnaround situations, or when performance is faltering or the CEO is failing to deliver on goals, executive sessions are about helping the company, the board, and the CEO get better.

At the end of the executive session, the Lead Director should crystallize the one or two (rarely as many as five) issues that seem to have importance. The twelve-month priorities could be a guide in determining which are most significant. But some topics will arise that are not on the board's list of priorities. The Lead Director should use his or her judgment about what items to communicate to the CEO. These could include questions the board would like the CEO to answer to validate the board's thinking or to fill a gap in their collective understanding of an issue.

Should the CEO Ever Be in the Room?

CEOs should be present for part of the executive session, for several reasons. For one thing, when directors discuss their ideas in the executive session, they often make assumptions—about the business, its leaders, the competition, or even how they think the CEO would answer a question—without having all the information they need. Perhaps a director, through her professional network, has come to know something about a player that is crossing industries and may emerge as a competitor, or is sensing that a technological breakthrough is coming from a nontraditional source. That information is worthy of discussion in the executive session, but chances are the CEO can add to it. The CEO might know the status of the competitor's research and have a view on what the competitive response is likely to be. The board needs to hear all of that to gauge the urgency of the issue.

The executive session is also a good venue to hear from the CEO what she needs from the board to help her perform better. Many boards miss this. The board should give the CEO an opportunity make requests or suggestions. It doesn't have to take more than a few minutes.

A third reason for the CEO to be present for part of the executive session is for the CEO and the board to brainstorm together. An emerging best practice is to use the informal setting of the executive session for the CEO to test out ideas with the board with no other managers present. The independent directors encourage the CEO to talk about whatever is on her mind and engage the board. Half-baked ideas are fine. The Lead Director of one board that uses executive sessions this way explains, "We tell the CEO to come into the executive session with us, and ask us a few questions. Bring us ideas and brainstorm with us. He's become comfortable doing that now."

It's a good idea to have the CEO present at the start of the meeting and available to answer questions periodically as the meeting progresses. While the CEO is present, the Lead Director can kick off a meeting by taking a few minutes to summarize his or her observations on the handful of things that are going well or on a few points from the last board meeting. In one executive session, there were four points, which laid the foundation for others to pose questions:

- A strategic dashboard created for the board was fabulous.
- The discussion of one division's people and the philosophy for compensating them was very rich.
- The CEO's addition of a strategic summary in the board book was useful.
- Pricing strategy would be a point of emphasis going forward.

After a short discussion of each point with the CEO, directors jumped in with other questions on their mind. "Given the upcoming election, will there be any changes in Washington that affect us materially?" was one question, for example, that required the CEO's perspective. After a half hour, they excused the CEO and continued the executive session without him. But the CEO remained available to answer more questions if any arose.

When the CEO is in the room, he of course gets the benefit of whatever insights emerge. In one executive session, the directors asked the CEO about candidates for the CFO job, which would be opening up soon when the incumbent retired. The CEO had two candidates in mind, one whose strength was internal operations, the other who was broader and more externally oriented. The CEO explained what he had in mind to develop each of them. In the course of the ensuing discussion, the board asked the CEO about the criteria he was using for the CFO job, and the CEO began to realize something he had overlooked.

The candidate who was internally focused was a superb accountant and had many other fine traits but was not quite a strategic mind. The other was weaker in accounting but knew the industry well and was a strategic thinker. The board pointed out that for those reasons, the second candidate might be able to be a CEO someday. The CEO had not considered that possibility. The directors made it clear that the CEO would make the final decision, but their identification of the candidate's CEO potential added a whole new dimension to the CEO's thinking.

How Do We Loop in the CEO After the Executive Session?

Several years ago, a CEO got feedback from the Lead Director that didn't sit right with him. He double-checked what he heard by asking another director, a close friend, and found out that the Lead Director hadn't given him the whole story. Such episodes adversely affect the trust that underpins the board-CEO relationship.

The Lead Director's feedback has to be communicated honestly and with the right nuance. Otherwise, the CEO senses the lack of transparency and is left to wonder what the real feedback is. Such things affect the relationship between the CEO and the board. It's a delicate task to maintain anonymity without arousing a sense of ambiguity in the CEO.

To be sure, not everything discussed in the executive session should be expressed to the CEO. Many topics are talked through and dropped because the directors decide they don't hold any weight. And other topics are issues that directors flag as potential warning signs, which they will watch as events unfold. In those cases, they should discuss what to tell the CEO—to convey areas for improvement without putting the CEO on the defensive. Several CEOs have been blindsided by their boards, because the boards gave no hints about their dissatisfaction. If boards are beginning to have doubts about their CEOs, they have to convey that truth well ahead of time and make suggestions for improvement, when possible.

Not all CEOs take criticism and bad news well, so feedback has to be given in a constructive way. If a board consensus is emerging in the executive session that the CEO is faltering, and that something will have to be done at some point, the CEO should not be left in the dark. The Lead Director must skillfully communicate that important message to the CEO. When a board decides to make a change, it should not be a surprise to the CEO.

The board must be very careful deciding not only what to convey to the CEO, but also when and how. It makes sense to fix the time and circumstances of the feedback, whether by phone or in meeting, in advance. It's usually preferable to deliver it verbally, rather than in writing, within 24 hours of the executive session.

One option is to have the Lead Director update the CEO one-on-one. In doing so, the Lead Director can answer questions and clarify the board's thinking, but he must listen well to the CEO's reaction, including the tone and nuances, so he can convey it accurately when he reports back to the board. Having a second director present can reduce the risk of inadvertently distorting the message or tone.

Another option is for the CEO to digest the feedback from the Lead Director, then talk to the independent directors as a group. He might say for instance, "I disagree with your point of view. Let me give you some more data around it. But I can do things differently even though we disagree."

When Should We Hold Executive Sessions?

In most cases, two or three executive sessions per year is about right. Their timing, however, seems to make a difference. Some boards are holding them before the board meeting instead of the more common practice of holding them after.

Executive sessions before meetings seem to help the board focus on the bigger picture. Granted, there are advantages in having an executive session after the board meeting, the greatest of which is that the issues will be fresh. Companies in turnaround, for instance, can quickly shift gears to discuss what they are picking up on and what to monitor while management's discussion is still hot on their minds.

But there are big downsides. For one thing, there is a tendency for directors to react to specifics they heard in the meeting just hours ago. They tend to zero in on operational details or on the presentations themselves, easily getting lost in the weeds. A second risk of holding executive sessions after board meetings is practical: after a long board meeting, many an independent director is in a hurry to catch a flight, and people tend to watch the clock. The time for executive sessions too often gets cut short. It starts with one director saying "I need to leave." Then the whole group begins to excuse itself.

When the executive session is held before the board meeting, directors come in with things they've reflected on. The Lead Director can build continuity by summarizing what they discussed at the last meeting. Under those circumstances, directors rarely nit-pick, and the executive session better serves its purpose of allowing higher-level, value-adding ideas and insights to emerge.

Key Points

- The executive session is the single best innovation for boards to own up.

- Conducted in the right way, executive sessions cement the CEO-board relationship. Conducted the wrong way, they strain it.

- Executive sessions must be informal enough for directors to raise any issue, but they cannot be allowed to devolve into unfounded criticism.

- The CEO should attend part of the executive session and be kept informed as the board's thinking evolves.

- Executive sessions better serve their purpose when they are held before board meetings.

Question 12.

HOW CAN OUR BOARD SELF-EVALUATION IMPROVE OUR FUNCTIONING AND OUR OUTPUT?

Over dinner a few years ago, an influential director said how proud he was of one of his boards. "We put in a lot of hard work," he explained. "I personally spent 250 hours on board work last year, including my committee work. And most of my fellow directors did about the same."

"That's terrific," I replied. "Sounds like you've made a real commitment to the company."

He knew I was doing research on corporate governance, so he wasn't surprised when I wanted to learn more: "Let me ask you something. What would you say are the one or two things your board did that really made a difference for the company?" The director took a long pause and looked up at the ceiling. He seemed lost in thought, like he was struggling to come up with a concrete answer. As I waited for him to respond, I realized that he probably had never thought about his board work in that way.

I have a strong belief that boards cannot gauge how well they are owning up unless they consider that question explicitly. The board's output—the quality of the decisions it makes and actions it takes—is the acid test of effective corporate governance. Does the board in fact help the CEO and the company perform better in the short- and long-term? When boards fail to consider their output, they can easily convince themselves and others that they're doing well when in fact the essence of their governance is weak. Directors should not confuse hard work, as commendable as it is, with meaningful results.

Boards are missing the point if they let their self-evaluations stop and start with the mechanics of how often they meet, for how long, and whether the chairman and CEO are separate. Those things are inputs. Even if such assessments meet external requirements, they're not very useful as a self-improvement tool. They don't distinguish between a board that delivers and one that is merely going through the motions. Boards that really want to improve their governance should use the evaluation process as a consistent practice to reflect on the *nature and quality of their output*, and with that in mind, determine what actions will make it better on a continuous basis.

Specify the Outputs

If directors are truly committed to good governance, they should explicitly state that the central purpose of their board self-evaluation process is to continuously improve their ability to govern effectively. The evaluation process must therefore be designed and conducted in a way that sheds light on whatever will take the board to the next level and improve the quality of its output.

Questionnaires, no matter how thoughtfully they are constructed and how comprehensive they try to be, don't capture the *nuances* of the board's actual workings and contribution. I have seen questionnaires containing as many as 70 items for directors to rank on a numerical scale. Those evaluations are burdensome for directors who are already strapped for time, but more to the point, they generally box in directors' thinking and fail to draw out their true feelings. The intricacies of board work are such that it is virtually impossible to anticipate every concern or issue board members might have and formulate a question around it. And asked open-ended questions, directors rarely write responses with the same precision that comes across in conversation.

A better process is to ask open-ended questions in one-on-one interviews conducted by the Lead Director, governance committee chair, or carefully chosen third party. The interviewer must understand the business and have great listening and synthesizing skills, sound and seasoned judgment, and a high degree of trust. The board must have total confidence in the person. Such people can be found; perhaps a retired board member or someone outside the board process altogether is a good choice.

Talking is different from writing. Provided anonymity is assured, it allows for more free-flowing discussion and gives directors more leeway to express whatever is on their mind. It also lets their passion and frustration come through. One highly effective and generally mild-mannered director became vocal and animated when he talked about the boardroom presentations. "Why can't they tell us in a clear, simple way what the issue is? Tell us the problem, what you're doing about it, what alternatives you've considered, and where you need help. I don't understand why people can't be clear and to the point." He returned to the same basic point several times during the evaluation interview.

Sometimes there's an issue lurking in the back of a director's mind. This process allows it to come to the surface. The person's tone of voice and choice of words often express subtleties that a skilled interviewer who knows the company well can detect and explore further. The opening question should prompt directors to describe the board's output by asking, for example, "Looking back at the last twelve months, with all the committee and board meetings, what three things did the board do especially well?" This immediately orients the person to think about what the board did or did not accomplish.

As directors reflect on the board's output, they should consider that there is often a time lag before the results are known. It may take two to four years to know whether the board selected the right CEO, for instance. Sometimes the board's contribution is an interim step toward a major output at a later date. Outlining a succession process and getting it started, for instance, is an important step toward selecting a CEO, which is probably the most important output of a board.

If nothing springs to mind, the interviewer can prompt the director: "How well do you think the board did in handling the pressure from a major investor to divest the company's real estate holdings?" or "What are your thoughts about how the board responded to the safety issues that came up this year?" or "How is the board doing on CEO succession?"

Boards can add or destroy value in many ways, but one of the chief ones is making decisions on what I call strategic bets. These are the big, risky decisions that change the trajectory of the business. It could be an acquisition or a major investment in a high-risk region, for example. Both Coke and Pepsi, two direct competitors for capital, have been trying to expand their markets for noncarbonated beverages. Coke turned down the decision to buy Quaker Oats and its Gatorade brand; Pepsi bought it and is now using the acquisition to branch into snacks. Reflection on whether the boards supported those strategic decisions and how they impacted the business could be very telling and prompt further reflection on whether the board had the right expertise or the right information to make those crucial judgments.

Shareholders want the board to make those kinds of judgments, and they want the board to be right most of the time. Self-evaluation is a time for boards to reflect on whether they weighed in on important items and how good their contributions really were. Directors, with perhaps a little prompting, should be able to identify them and comment on them.

I ran into the Lead Director of one consumer company, for example, who cut right to the chase. His board's output—in this case the decision to not back the previous CEO's recommendation to seek a private equity buyer—was costly. "We should have listened to our previous CEO," he said.

In his eight-year tenure, that CEO had brought his company to a new high in part by expanding the number of brands. As his retirement neared, he recommended that the company seek a private equity buyer, because he felt conditions were right for shareholders to reap the benefit of the company's strong position. The board considered the option at length but one director wasn't sold on it. He had had experience in a similar industry and had rifts with the CEO from time to time, creating distrust between the two of them. This director thought the CEO's stock options might be affecting his decision to pursue a buyer, and persuaded the rest of the board to forgo selling the business to private equity.

Six months later the CEO retired, and the board brought on a young, aggressive, and very smart leader who had considerable success building brands as the division head of a larger company in a different industry, a background not unlike that of the retired CEO. After evaluating the strategy, the CEO decided to change tack, with the board's full agreement, just as the company's markets started to nosedive. The combination of a new strategy and declining markets cut the stock price 50 percent within a year of the new CEO's arrival. This was before the financial crisis in 2008. Unfortunately, the private equity option was no longer on the table, partly because the company's key market was tightening and partly because private equity's purchasing appetite had by then almost vanished. The board's window of opportunity had closed.

It's important to recognize the smaller contributions boards make as well, and the interviewer can explicitly ask about these. At every board meeting and in every communication with management, directors should be exploring ideas with the CEO and making their expertise, insights, and viewpoints available to management. One director casually suggested a shift to economic value added (EVA) to rationalize its portfolio of products and customer segments. His reasoning got the CEO interested in making the change, and the director connected the CEO with top experts to help implement it. With a better tool for resource allocation, the company subsequently reduced customer segments and products, sharpening its focus and laying the foundation to improve its return on invested capital. Before the company adopted this tool, division management had been pursuing growth in subsegments that were unprofitable and cash inefficient.

Here are some other specific outputs I've seen boards generate:

- In early 2008, months before the havoc on Wall Street, several directors with capital markets experience advised management on short-term debt. The CFO believed interest rates were headed down and felt he could save 20 to 30 basis points by waiting to secure short-term debt. But one director said he saw tightening in the capital markets. Two of his peers confirmed his observation. After some discussion, the board persuaded the CFO that it was worth the extra basis points to avoid liquidity risk. As 2008 unfolded, that decision proved to be a good one.

- In a business review shortly after three new directors joined the board, the board launched a discussion about the smallest of the company's four divisions, which had been sputtering for three or four years. Some directors questioned whether it should even be part of the company, but after some research, the board agreed that yes, it belonged. Next the CEO asked the head of the division and two of his direct reports to report on the business to the board. During that presentation the directors noticed that the head of the division seemed psychologically tired. Maybe the division needed new leadership. They noticed that one of the direct reports seemed especially capable. The CEO confirmed that was true, and after some consideration, made the change. The new leader turned the division around within a year.

- One director took it upon himself to coach the CEO on the pacing of new product introductions. There were too many products coming online, and the sales force wasn't big enough to handle them. The CEO got the message and worked with his team to manage the pace.

- A director coached the CEO to think not just in terms of revenues but in terms of market value. The company's P/E ratio was 12; its best competitor's was 18. That comment gave the CEO a new way to think about growth, and he started searching for ways to close the gap.

- In a boardroom discussion in January 2008, one director, who has a vast network on Wall Street, informed management and the board that the CFOs of a number of companies were making a flight to quality, meaning they were converting their cash investments from normal paper to U.S. Treasuries. He indicated this was the harbinger of an important event to take place. The board urged the CEO to de-leverage fast to avoid a cash crunch.

Directors might find it hard to specify the board's output the first time they're asked. The CEO, however, might have an easier time responding, and his or her perspective should be heavily weighted. At the end of the day, the CEO and the senior team are the recipients of the board's output. So ask how the CEO sees it. What items had gravitas, even if they weren't eventually adopted? What comments led her to reorient her thinking on external conditions? Did the board make her "smarter?" A best practice that has emerged at Tyco Electronics is to ask the CEO, CFO, and other managers who interact with the board and board committees to give their individual views on what the board does well and needs to do better and offer suggestions for each committee and board member going forward. That feedback is compiled separately from the board self-evaluation.

Room for Improvement

The whole self-evaluation exercise becomes much more powerful when the facilitator helps directors connect the board's output (or lack thereof) with specific changes in board composition or practices. When members of one board noted that the company's supply chain problem was an issue the board had yet to address, the facilitator prompted directors to think about what it would take to make a contribution in that area. The company had built a supply chain in the 1990s centered in Chongqing in southwest China. With costs rising and the Chinese pushing production to the northwest, the supply chain was becoming uncompetitive. The issue was troubling to the directors.

After drawing out their concerns, the facilitator phrased a follow-up question in a way that would allow directors to reach their own conclusions about how they might resolve it, saying, "What kinds of things would help the board if it were to take up this issue in the coming year?" Several directors noted that no one on the board had any supply chain expertise, and perhaps it would be helpful if they recruited someone with that background. Within a few months, the board did recruit such a director, and he subsequently worked with management to make significant improvements.

Another board was proud that it had helped the company change its capital structure. When the facilitator asked, "Do you have any thoughts about how the board can make more contributions at this level?" one director noted that one of his colleagues had done the bulk of the work and was at risk of being overloaded. He added, "We should get another director with experience in capital markets so [Ruth] doesn't have to carry all the weight." It's a good idea for the interviewer to ask about specific topics such as committees, board agenda, meetings, and composition as well to be sure directors don't miss anything. Here again, open-ended questions work best. Questions might include the following:

- Does the board spend sufficient time on the three to five most important items on the agenda during the year? (Many boards still do not use a twelve-month priorities list.)

- How is the use of time in board meetings? ("Too many PowerPoint slides, not enough time for discussion!" is a common complaint.)
- Do you have any comments on the information packages or presentations you get from management?
- Does the board have the right committees, and are they functioning well?
- Does the board have the right kind of expertise? Is anything missing?
- If the board adopted a new process recently, say it implemented a twelve-month priorities list, the interviewer should specifically ask about it.

It's always a good idea to ask about board leadership and board dynamics because that's how the best judgments of the group emerge. How good was the debate on big issues? Did all the points of view come out? Did the board focus on the right questions? Was the Lead Director effective in getting all the viewpoints out while still getting closure? The particular fixes are less important at this point, although some directors might have suggestions.

It helps if directors have the opening questions ahead of time so they can give them some thought. If they trust the interviewer, they will be candid, sometimes surprisingly so. The skill is for the interviewer to provide just enough context for directors to share their minds, without leading the witness. In subsequent self-evaluations, particularly when directors see how powerful the results can be, they cut to the chase— "I question whether this company will ever make the cost of capital" or "I'm not comfortable with our succession plan." The process becomes both efficient and effective in gathering the board's deepest, most pointed concerns, paving the way for the board's continuous improvement.

Given the right line of questioning, directors often make their own connections between board practices and board output. For example, a director who comments on what a great contribution the board made during a recent strategy session might relate it to the board agenda later in the interview, saying: "We need to set aside time in June for a follow up on the strategy."

Results and Follow-Through

Interviewing a dozen or so directors and a CEO generates a lot of information. The interviews have nuances and inflections, and not all the responses will be consistent. The facilitator has to capture those nuances and carefully define the centers of gravity. This is where the interviewer must demonstrate wise judgment and the ability to synthesize sometimes disparate comments. He or she should check that judgment with the governance committee chair, the Lead Director, and perhaps the CEO. They can then decide together how to go forward with input to the board.

There might be particular sensitivities that could lead the governance committee to exclude a point raised by a director. For example, a director at one company recommended that the company split the chair and CEO roles. But the governance committee knew that the issue had been fully debated and that one director would not change her position, despite the fact that her colleagues disagreed with her. Reopening the issue would be a waste of time. One director preceded his comment by saying, "I know the CEO won't like it, but he needs to know. . . ." The governance committee chair mulled over that piece of feedback and decided to approach the CEO privately on that issue.

The facilitator should summarize the findings for the board, being careful not to reveal who said what. A more complete set of comments, without attribution, can be included in an appendix. In doing so, the idea is not to reach hard and fast conclusions or to make firm recommendations; the board will do that for itself. Rather, the initial processing should cull out the most important issues and distill the interviews so the board can easily digest them. The results should be presented in executive session, and the board should take time to discuss them and decide on next steps.

GE conducts an open-ended, interview-type board self-evaluation each December, following a review of its overall governance and risk processes in the fall. Results of the self-evaluation are presented to the independent directors usually during their executive session breakfast meeting. CEO Jeff Immelt is present for part of it, and general counsel Brackett Denniston attends as needed. The board translates the findings into a list of actions that get incorporated into board, committee, or management agendas and get followed up on throughout the year. Directors describe that discussion as being highly energizing, interactive, and candid. Denniston notes, "Directors are convinced that things come up during the self-evaluation and discussion that might not come out in a questionnaire. They are more communicative as a result of being completely comfortable with the process." After a full discussion of the board's contributions and other results of the evaluation, the board can begin to articulate and prioritize action items—and there are always action items.

The chair of the governance committee or Lead Director should ensure the action items are clear and revisit them to be sure whatever was agreed on is being executed. The action items often become incorporated into the twelve-month agenda.

After its evaluation, one board decided that (1) the company strategy needed to be reviewed, (2) the board wanted to be fully engaged in the process of recruiting a particular direct report to the CEO, and (3) the board wanted to be kept apprised of how the CEO was handling a customer on whom 15 percent of revenues depended. If there are lots of points to follow up on, they can be delegated to committees.

This type of self-evaluation raises the board's awareness of what they are or should be contributing, which in itself tends to change the board's behavior. But it also points to specific necessary changes in board practices and composition. Those two things combined help the board perform better.

The Importance of Peer Evaluation

Many boards are reluctant to do a peer review, but it is a very valuable instrument for improving corporate governance. In many cases, directors are reluctant to review their peers not because they're afraid of what they'll hear about themselves, but rather, because they prefer not to criticize their colleagues. Directors should come to terms with their hesitation, because peer evaluation can keep the board dynamics in balance. It is the best way to encourage directors to contribute more and to point out behaviors that can be corrected.

Peer review is also a great tool for helping the Lead Director or governance committee chair deal with a director who has become such a problem that directors no longer want that person on the board. Like all groups of human beings, boards sometimes have a member who continually stymies productive discussion and won't listen to others, or who damages the board-management relationship, say, by continually making unreasonable requests. Other directors roll their eyes when he begins to speak.

Boards cannot afford to let such problems persist. Although peer review should never be undertaken specifically to remove particular board members, it may sometimes have that effect, to the betterment of corporate governance. The review makes it much less personal for the Lead Director or chair of the governance committee to approach that person. The governance committee and Lead Director should have their antennae up all the time for signs of dysfunctional behavior, but peer review validates their perceptions.

The peer review should focus on directors' contributions. Ask, for instance, whether the board member asked a profound question or made a profound suggestion, or whether the person moved management forward in its thinking and deliberations. Comments like these are telling: "He's always thinking two steps ahead of everyone else," or "she reframes discussions in a way that opens my eyes to new possibilities." Such feedback reinforces directors' participation.

If there are problems, they will come out, provided the setting is private and the interviewer is highly trusted: "He's really smart, but he doesn't understand the business," or "Every once in awhile, she gets into the weeds on something that could really be taken offline," or "He doesn't speak up much." A director might say a dozen good things about someone, but just drop in a hint of a negative: "Charlie is very smart and articulate. I really like him. He knows so much about the debt markets." Then toward the end of her comment, the director might say, "At the last meeting, he led a discussion about structured investment vehicles for an hour. I learned a lot although it didn't end up being particularly relevant." In other words, her fellow director was side-tracking. It takes a keen listening ear to pick up on that code and careful judgment to sift through to something useful that directors are reluctant to express.

There is a world of difference between directors who have room to improve but are valued by their colleagues and *unwanted* directors who disrupt the board. There is also a sharp distinction between a *dissenting* director who earns respect by asking the tough questions and pushing the board's thinking and a director who is simply contentious and stubborn. For the most part, directors know the difference, and it will come out in a peer review.

The results of a peer review should be presented to the individual director by the Lead Director or governance committee chair or both. One board has the chairman and Lead Director sit with each director, and that too is working well. Most directors love the feedback, as long as it is presented constructively. They realize that even the best of them have room for improvement. Negative feedback can be framed by saying, "We're asking everyone for suggestions for how each of us can help take the board to the next level. . . ."

Things are stickier for directors who are clearly unwanted, but when presented with evidence of how the rest of the board sees it, few directors will choose to stay. One way that is in vogue now to proceed without triggering a round of SEC filings explaining the cause for resignation is to suggest that the director simply not stand for renomination. That worked well for one diversified Fortune 500 company when an independent director's boardroom and public behavior changed after some troubling personal problems. The director became irritable in the boardroom and began shooting his mouth off in public, and other members started to complain. The Lead Director began discussions with the director two months before he was up for renomination, allowing enough time for the director to make a smooth transition and save face. Don't forget to celebrate the departing director for the contributions he or she has made.

Key Points

- Focus on the board's output, and seek the CEO's opinion. Is the board really making a contribution to the business?
- Interviews by the Lead Director, chair of the governance committee, or a trusted third-party allow more nuance on the board's functioning to surface.
- It's up to the governance committee to ensure the board identifies action items and follows through to continuously improve.
- Peer evaluation is a chance to reinforce positive behavior and get at issues that are difficult to raise.

Question 13.

HOW DO WE STOP FROM MICROMANAGING?

CEOs for the most part accept the board as their boss and as a valuable sounding board and source of input. But they don't always get what they're looking for from their boards. A common complaint among chief executives is that directors get into the weeds, digging into operational details that have little strategic value. "I have to be polite and respect them," said one CEO. "But it's very time consuming and nobody gets anything out of it. Sometimes one director consumes a lot of airtime right at the start of a four-hour board meeting, and for the rest of the meeting the discussion never lifts to a higher altitude."

In one board meeting for a services company, for example, during a quarterly company performance review, a division head mentioned a number of new contracts they had signed, including one for a project in the northern part of China. That caught the attention of one director, who happened to be knowledgeable and interested in that geographic area, and he started asking about the specifics of the contract: Are you delivering this contract alone or are you partnering with someone? What has been the history of the partnership? Another director joined in. There was nothing unusual about the contract from a business perspective; it didn't entail a lot of risk, and at $3 million in a $2 billion company, it was not particularly large. Management answered all the directors' questions, but it took thirty minutes for the line of inquiry to run its course. Meanwhile, the questioning was not of interest to the other board members, who lost their concentration and started checking their Blackberries. The meeting lost energy and the questioning went nowhere.

It's a common pattern for one director to raise a question and then for one or two other directors to pile on. Before long, a handful of directors are getting into minutiae, and the whole board dynamic is derailed. The danger of course is that it takes the focus off more serious issues like strategy, perception of external trends, succession, and enterprise risk.

Such micromanaging also puts CEOs on the defensive and makes them less effective. In today's corporate governance environment, CEOs are often reluctant to push back. One director asked his CEO to conduct a study on how the cost of capital was calculated in related industries. The CEO obliged, but it distracted the management team and probably cost a couple hundred thousand dollars to research. In the end, nothing changed.

Micromanaging simply cannot be tolerated. Boards have to understand what it is and what it does to their effectiveness, and each and every director must take part in controlling it. I've seen directors roll their eyes when their peers start in, but rarely do they intervene, even as they complain that the board doesn't spend enough time on the things that matter. Directors must take responsibility for managing the board's time. As much as management complains about the problem of micromanaging, they may be contributing to it by providing too many slides and unnecessary details. The CEO and the senior team have a role to play in shaping the nature of the board's output and the altitude of the discussion.

What Is—and Isn't—Micromanaging?

The difference between micromanaging and appropriate questioning is not always a bright line. What really defines micromanaging is not whether a director is digging into details. It's really a question of which details and for what purpose. Is the director making a small point, like nit-picking expenses? Or is the director drilling down into details that help reveal a higher-level issue—detecting a structural change, getting at the root cause of a problem, or questioning the effectiveness of a process?

Asking questions of an operating nature is not in itself micromanaging, as long as the questions lead to insights about issues like strategy, performance, major investment decisions, key personnel, the choice of goals, or risk assessment. Probing a decline in gross margins, for example, can easily be seen as nit-picky in some circumstances. But in industries like office supplies or personal computers, where gross margins have taken a beating over the last ten years, directors might be trying to discern whether the decline is symptomatic of a fundamental shift in the industry and therefore whether the strategy has become obsolete. The key lies in the analytics of working backward to link the operating details with strategic issues.

For a mobile phone operator, subscriber churn rate is an operating detail with very strategic importance. The board of a telecommunications company that approves a multibillion-dollar project to lay new cable has a stake in knowing how the implementation is going. The project's success might depend heavily on assumptions management made about attracting and retaining targeted high-revenue customers. The board will want to dig into details about how many customers are willing to pay a premium for voice, video, and text combined. Are a sufficient number of customers coming on line on schedule? What percentage is staying with the company? What is the monthly churn, or turnover, in customers and what is the average customer bill? These operational details are an important lens for tracking the execution of the strategy and gauging whether it is working. These items materially affect the business going forward.

When a director picks up on a small point and challenges it for the sake of showing who is right or what could have been done differently, or when a director attempts to make a decision about operations, or individual people, it's fair to say that person is micromanaging. This typically happens in the area of the director's expertise and is driven by a personal need to demonstrate superior subject knowledge.

How a line of questioning is worded can also indicate whether a director is micromanaging. The difference lies in how the CEO could respond. Does the inquiry put the CEO in a box, as opposed to shedding light on a subject and opening the door for a richer discussion? Let me give you an example. In the middle of 2007, most boards across the globe were keen to learn how management was responding to the steep rise in commodity prices and the impact on margins. Many boards debated the potential impact on margins and what could or could not be passed on to customers. That was a vital discussion to have. Directors who had to increase prices at some point in their careers know how difficult it is to sit face to face with a customer when the management had not increased prices for ten years.

A micromanaging director might initiate the discussion of pricing by lecturing on her personal experience in dealing with a price increase, implying that the CEO lacks the courage to address the issue and that he should do exactly as the director had done. The implication is that management can do it if it has the will.

A different approach to the topic is to say, "I'm curious about several aspects of inflation and our pricing strategy. What is our process of adjusting prices as inflationary conditions change? How are decisions initiated? Who gets involved and with what tools? What training is being given to people who are looking at pricing and to the sales force that brings it all home? Are the regional sales managers buying into it?" This lets management explain what the company is doing and what alternatives it has considered, an explanation that might include things the director didn't think of, like issuing a press release.

The director could then ask, "What benchmarking are you doing to improve pricing processes and reduce our exposure to margin compression? Are there any strategic implications that the board needs to learn about?" In that way, the director opens the door to several possibilities without insisting on his pet course of action. It opens the door for other directors to join the discussion. This kind of questioning becomes an imperative when the company is highly leveraged and commodities prices increase several times in a year. It gives directors insight into whether the company has the organizational mechanisms to move and is not awaiting orders from the top.

The difference in approach has a profound impact on the boardroom dynamic. Asking questions at the right altitude, with the right tone, and about the right things refocuses management's attention while respecting the CEO's decision-making authority. It is, after all, management's job to deal with the margin compression and decide on its pricing practices, not the board's. The board is there to make sure management has a plan and that it is executing that plan.

How Can Directors Curb Micromanaging?

Making micromanaging part of the board evaluation and, in particular, of a peer review reminds directors that they are there to govern, not run the business, and can help directors curb the impulse. But not all directors are self-aware. Then it's up to the board's leaders, the CEO, and other directors to control it, change behaviors, and keep the dialogue on track.

When micromanaging occurs, the Lead Director or non-executive chair has to take charge. After one director started badgering a company's IT director about its systems, the board's Lead Director stepped in and joked, "Hey (Joe), are you looking for a job in IT?" The tone was collegial and humorous, but the director got the point. More Lead Directors should take that kind of initiative to gently pull the dialogue out of a micromanager's rabbit hole. They can't defer to know-it-all directors, even on topics of their expertise, or else the micromanaging will continue. Pushing back against micromanaging requires a lot of sensitivity to board dynamics—a key skill for the Lead Director.

It also helps when the board has agreed upon the twelve-month priorities, and is clear about the strategy and the milestones. Having a dashboard that individual directors can use to monitor progress on critical issues on their own also helps board meetings stay on point. During difficult times, such as during a turnaround, a dashboard can help the board hold its nerve and stay focused on the big picture until the business turns the corner.

One board wondered whether the company's cost reductions were sufficient after it saw margins shrink in the midst of a turnaround. They drilled the VP of logistics for two hours on different aspects of procurement—how many suppliers do we have? Why so many? Your transport costs look high compared to my company's; what benchmarks are you looking at? How are you factoring in oil prices? But I wouldn't call that micromanaging. These were vital operational questions that were core to the success of the turnaround strategy. The VP stood his ground and could address all the questions. In the end, they decided together that the logistics goals were not ambitious enough. They created new goals and a dashboard of measures to track them, and the VP starting delivering improved numbers the very next quarter. The board never had to do a deep dive on the subject again, and the VP never lost motivation. Let's not forget that business leaders below the CEO appreciate when directors are being constructive and value the opportunity to learn from them.

Every board evaluation should include a question about whether the board is micromanaging, and the CEO and management team should have the chance to respond. A peer review also provides the opportunity for directors to give their colleagues feedback about their micromanaging. When the committee chair, Lead Director, or both present the feedback in a private conversation, most directors get the message and will adjust their behavior. (For a fuller discussion of board self-evaluation and peer review, see Chapter Twelve.)

A director who continually challenges the CEO might do so because, for example, the overheads are too high. A seasoned board leader can make that distinction by talking with the director. There might be a simple way to rectify the problem—by conducting a session on overheads or suggesting the director meet privately with the CEO and his team—to stop the micromanaging.

The worst thing to happen to a board is when the CEO and the management team lose respect for the board. I found this to quite often be the case in my research. The Lead Director needs to be sensitive to it.

How Can the CEO Keep the Board from Micromanaging?

CEOs don't realize that they bring some of the micromanaging on themselves with their presentations to the board. Walking the board through highly detailed quarterly performance numbers without orienting directors to the most critical outcomes and causes is an open invitation to micromanage. If the CFO or other direct reports present one mind-numbing slide after another, board members are going to jump in and ask questions to try to make some kind of contribution. In the name of politeness, management will field the questions, without interruption, while bigger items get pushed back on the agenda.

During one such presentation, one director, the CEO of a very large corporation, took out his calculator to reconcile the numbers from three slides and spent a good deal of the board's time on an inconsequential discrepancy he found. In this case, the director, an academic, repeated it three times and demanded an explanation. The minutes ticked by and the board barely got to its review of key personnel, the most important item on that meeting's agenda.

The CEO should work with the board to create an information architecture that leads the board toward meaty discussions of vital issues. The best way to do that is to be direct. In each presentation, the CEO or whoever the presenter is can tell the board up-front what he or she needs the board to focus on. In fact, the CEO should coach presenters to take that approach and start their presentations by saying, "I'd really like your input on x and y." Addressing strategic topics first puts directors at the right altitude for the entire meeting.

Another best practice is for the CEO and other presenters to give the bad news on the first page in unmistakable terms, then describe the whys and the context. Say a financial services company that depends on its consumer business is reporting flat performance for the quarter. Management of the division might hit the low points directly: "The first bit of bad news is that there have been higher delinquencies in credit cards and given the state of the economy, that's likely to continue. Second, a super-regional bank doubled its advertising so our share of new card issuance has taken a beating." Then the division manager presents what actions she'll undertake.

When it comes to boardroom discussions, the CEO must participate as a member of the board and a peer and not sit passively. He or she has more information and subject knowledge than any director and therefore should not permit the board to draw the wrong inferences. If the Lead Director does not intervene when the line of questioning crosses into micromanaging, the CEO can in her own respectful, courteous way ask other directors for their viewpoints on the same issue. Someone is likely to pick up the cue and raise the dialogue to a higher level. A CEO could say, for example: "We can go into how we calculated productivity if you all think it's worthwhile, but I can assure you the formula has been applied consistently. Do you think it's worth it?" With that prompt, nine times out of ten another director will speak up and back off the line of questioning—and end the micromanaging.

Key Points

- Micromanaging drains energy and makes the board and management less effective.

- *Why* a director is drilling for details and *how* the questions are asked make a difference.

- The Lead Director plays a pivotal role in shaping dialogue when micromanaging begins to creep in. But other directors should help keep their peers from micromanaging.

- Use evaluations to pinpoint whether micromanaging is becoming a problem, and to align the board on how to minimize it.

- Management reduces micromanaging when presentations are well structured and at the right level.

Question 14.

HOW PREPARED ARE WE TO WORK WITH ACTIVIST SHAREHOLDERS AND THEIR PROXIES?

Shareholders are the real boss—the sooner boards realize this fact and live up to their obligation to represent them, the better. And just as directors in general became more active and engaged in their companies after Sarbanes-Oxley was passed, so have shareholders. That activism is not going to go away, and because of it some boards are in the line of fire.

Your performance as a board will increasingly be scrutinized, as much as the company's performance. And it won't just be by Wall Street analysts and institutional investors. Anybody who owns a share has access not only to information about the company but also to public forums on which to talk about the company. Bloggers search through the footnotes of SEC filings. Seventy-eight-year-old women with no corporate leadership experience file shareholder proxies and end up interviewed on business channels.

Many more shareholders are searching for gaps in a company's potential and its achievement and don't hesitate to rattle management and the board when they find them. Every shareholder, even the day-trader, can influence the future of the company. So every shareholder matters. Among them, a special class of investors is putting their money where their mouth is. They are taking the opposite of voting with their wallets, whereby they would sell stock when they didn't like what they see. Rather, these investors are buying shares and asking for board seats.

Boards have to adapt to the reality that shareholder activism is here to stay. They should be prepared to communicate directly with shareholders under certain circumstances, and work to understand and perhaps make use of investors' analysis. They should realize that having an investor representative on the board is not the end of the world; investor-nominated directors often become a constructive force and colleagues with valuable ideas. And while the shareholder proxies that rate board performance may have incomplete information, they often raise legitimate concerns that boards must address.

Opening the Lines of Communication with Shareholders

Communication is central to resolving issues between two or more parties, so boards should actively open up lines of communication. In the past, all communications went through the CEO/chair, and that is still appropriate most of the time. But there are also circumstances when directors have to directly hear shareholders' complaints and concerns. Even if they don't agree with them all, they have to demonstrate that they are listening and respond with honesty about what the board is thinking and planning to do. When management's credibility has been lost or is in question, a direct line from shareholders to the board becomes even more vital.

Boards should set up processes to govern those communications in advance of extraordinary circumstances. Having every director field calls from any shareholder is chaotic and potentially dangerous if, for instance, different directors convey different messages. Rather, boards should name a primary contact for shareholders, typically the Lead Director or nonexecutive chair, and set ground rules over what is to be discussed with whom. And they must have guidelines that cover informal contacts that individual directors may have with investors, for example, with clear guidelines to report back to the board if directors are approached about company business.

Perhaps the most talked-about example of a board meeting with its ultimate bosses happened at Home Depot. When directors skipped the 2006 annual meeting, several shareholder groups, already on edge after several years of a flat stock price, were upset that they did not have the opportunity to voice their displeasure with CEO Bob Nardelli's compensation package. They requested to meet with Bonnie Hill, chair of the Compensation Committee, to express their concerns. She was willing to meet with them, and the board and the company agreed that the meetings should take place. As Hill says, "We felt it was the right thing to do; it was our responsibility and obligation to meet with shareholders."

Hill worked with Home Depot's investor relations, human resources, and legal departments to set up face-to-face meetings with organizations including CalPERS, the AFL-CIO, ISS, and the Council of Institutional Investors. The meeting schedule began shortly after the May 2006 annual meeting and continued through the end of the year.

When Nardelli resigned in January of 2007, his exit package, estimated at $210 million, was widely ridiculed in the press. Shareholders were less riled up; they already knew what the package would be (it had been negotiated when Nardelli was hired in 2000 and had been disclosed in the proxy). Still, compensation remained a hot button, and new CEO Frank Blake knew it. When the board appointed Blake to succeed Nardelli, his first statement was that he did not want his compensation to be a source of distraction for the company; he wanted to get the company focused on the business at hand. That attitude was a wonderful breath of fresh air, and the Compensation Committee worked with Blake to structure a package that was 89 percent at risk and aligned with shareholders' interests (Blake had pushed to have 90 percent at risk; 89 percent was the compromise).

Once Blake's compensation had been set and announced, Hill, along with investor relations, made personal phone calls to the organizations that she and others at Home Depot had spoken with previously to answer any questions they might have. Shareholders complimented Blake's package and Blake himself as a CEO who "got it." In that short period of time, Home Depot went from being what some considered worst in class to best in class in executive compensation.

On those calls, Hill and her colleagues listened carefully to constituents' concerns, took many into serious consideration, but didn't act on every point. When the board disagreed, she said so. "They put out their views and things they wanted us to do," Hill said. "And we responded, 'Here are some things we'll take back and consider. And here are some other things that go against the grain of where we believe we should be and what we believe is in the best interest of shareholders.'" The intellectual honesty built a lot of trust. As the various organizations saw the deep thought and diligence behind the board's points of view, they came to respect that directors and management were making thoughtful decisions.

When questions came up about the board election process and other governance practices, Hill felt they needed to be addressed with equal forthrightness. She spoke with Ken Langone, then the chair of the Nominating and Corporate Governance Committee, who enthusiastically volunteered to have that committee meet with all shareholders in an open town hall meeting. This type of open forum was a bold and unprecedented step in a genuine effort to repair shareholder relations.

At the town hall, Langone opened simply by saying, "We're here to answer your questions." That immediately set the tone. For two hours, four directors answered questions about the nominating process, the retirement schedule, and a host of other governance practices. There were even a number of financial questions, and the directors answered the ones they could with information that was in the public domain. The entire meeting was very congenial, an open discussion with very little arguing. Institutional investors, unions, and shareholder advocates who were at the meeting gave it high marks. It made a world of difference to Home Depot shareholder relations.

I am not suggesting that boards should routinely set up conference calls and town hall meetings with shareholders. It really depends on the circumstances. Different types of shareholders, for example, might require different levels of engagement. But the board must have in its repertoire some options for constructive dialogue with the owners of the business and must be flexible in keeping the lines open.

Seeing Through the Eyes of Activist Shareholders

When activist shareholders come calling, boards should not automatically brush them off as fast-buck corporate raiders, as many have done in the past. Those investors may have spotted a genuine blind spot that management and the board missed. Activist investors often bring very detailed financial analyses—for example, a rigorous benchmarking that demonstrates how much of a difference modern tools can make in boosting margins through supply chain improvements—that are real eye-openers for the board and management.

Activist investors for the most part really do have shareholder value in mind. Their conclusions may be wrong, but you need to deal with the substance of what they have to say to figure that out. As unpleasant as the experiences were, for example, companies like Time Warner, Heinz, Motorola, and Mattel could have all benefited from the proposals and analyses that activist investors brought to their boards. Instead, they suffered through acrimonious public exchanges and negative public relations. In most of those cases shareholder value declined, and in some instances the decline has been so deep that there is little hope of recovery. Activist investors push management for a variety of actions, of course. Generally speaking, they tend to focus on three areas:

- **Improving finance and operations.** Some investors have a great deal of operational expertise on staff and hire consultants to develop more information. They have the analytical expertise to zero in on resource allocation, merger integration, capital structure, or supply chain operations, for example, and build compelling arguments for action. In some cases, they build positive relationships with directors and top management over several years before they are convinced to buy a significant stake and present their cases. Boards can often benefit greatly from these diagnostic insights.

- **Unlocking asset value.** Another class of investor tends to focus on unlocking value through portfolio re-arrangement. They are often able to see that the value of a business unit, a technology, or some other asset is higher for somebody else than it is for the company. Sometimes they see that the value of an asset is nearing a peak and should therefore be unloaded now. This perspective can be very valuable for boards to hear out, but they should be wary that some investors are looking to make a fast buck and may not have long-term interests in mind.

- **Changing management.** Some activists believe the management team is not right for the job or can't execute, and boards have to understand the investors' underlying motivations. Perhaps a past conflict might be influencing the current relationship. Or perhaps management might not be doing a good enough job communicating with investors. Boards should get below the surface to see whether there is any substance to the argument.

I have four pieces of advice for boards when activist investors come calling. This advice comes from my interviews with several highly regarded directors of public companies. It is con-tra to what had been practiced only a few years earlier. First, don't be surprised that many credible investors come to boards with open minds and constructive concerns. "When we met with [several investor groups], I initially thought those meetings would be relatively hostile," says Hill. "I have to say that was just not the case. We sat across the table and had very civil discussions. They would raise their points. We would give the company's and the board's perspective. There were a number of things we took into consideration. And we had issues that we agreed to disagree about because that's the way it was."

Second, avoid knee-jerk reactions based on the assumption that investors are right. Look at the issue from investors' view-points, not just through management's eyes. But be prepared to defend a CEO who is missing the numbers for good reason, even if shareholders are discontent with management's performance. The board must be crystal clear about the causes for missing the numbers. It is the board's responsibility to know, and to make clear its rationale for sticking up for their CEO. Cisco Systems did that with CEO John Chambers, and the board's judgment to back Chambers despite shareholder complaints was borne out by results later.

Third, in dealing with investors' concerns, boards need to understand their motivation and intent. What are the investor's holdings? What is the investor's time horizon? What has the investor done in other companies? A long-term investor who identifies a strategic flaw, like a long-term project that is failing and needs to be cut off because conditions have changed, is very different from an arbitrageur who holds warrants in a potential takeover target.

Fourth, a board should validate the elements of the concern through third parties and rigorous research. Would a break-up of Motorola into four pieces really be a benefit to shareholders? The board should seek expert advice before accepting or reject-ing the argument. It should bring on advisors of its own.

Boards face a huge dilemma in dealing with activist investors in the context of the global financial meltdown. As gummed up liquidity flows drive a dreadful decline in the market value of certain assets, active investors are forcing some companies to make major shifts in their portfolios. It is tough for boards to divest an asset with perfectly good long-term value because of the dynamics of the capital markets while cash-rich investors wait like vultures to grab valuable assets dirt cheap.

Working with Investor-Nominated Directors on the Board

Boards also need to deal with the fear that having shareholders gain seats on the board will destroy the chemistry and paralyze the board. "It's taken us a long time to build the rapport on our board," one director complained. "And now some investor who doesn't know anything about the business is going to come on the board like a bull in a china shop. How are we going to get anything done?"

Activist investors generally don't ask for board seats unless the company hasn't delivered for a few years. They prefer not to take a board seat because it limits their liquidity options. Thus, most activist investors prefer to speak their minds behind the scenes.

Some investor-nominated directors earn their board seats through shareholder proxy vote campaigns. Other times, a public campaign to agitate for change starts to influence the investor community, the media, and even customers and suppliers. It could become a frenzy, as happened at Yahoo! in early 2008. When the pressures get too great, the board needs to consider relenting in order to quiet things down, even if it means giving in to the activist.

Many times, investor-nominated directors have made a positive difference after joining a board. Boards need to know that many activist investors have earned a lot of respect from board members by doing superb financial analysis that gets to the heart of a thorny issue. In some cases, a few directors on the board had the same idea, although their board's group dynamics had not gelled well enough for the solution to become a consensus. "I knew in my gut that the proposal was right all along," one director said about the divestiture that an activist had lobbied for. "The analyses he brought really confirmed it."

Their solutions can be challenging, but sometimes that's exactly what the board needs to hear. An investor might do a deep dive into resource allocation, for example, using a framework the board has not seen. Combining modern analytics with proprietary benchmarks, the investor might demonstrate that the returns on incremental capital over three years have trailed the cost of capital, therefore destroying shareholder value. That kind of analysis can be a real eye-opener, even for good leaders of very large companies. I have heard two CEOs of multibillion-dollar companies say, "We don't have the expertise or resources to do that analysis in house." The analyses were so illuminating that both CEOs subsequently built that capability in-house.

Boards need to be cognizant that one or two directors can change the board's group dynamics constructively, although it may take some time to develop a comfort level. According to Ralph Whitworth, principal of Relational Investors and veteran of many boards, as long as the new director is professional and constructive and has the knowledge needed to serve on the board, it doesn't take that long.

"A very good example of this," Whitworth says, "was when I went on the Tektronix board. A few days before I joined the board, they announced that their CEO Jerry Meyer was going to retire and stay on as chair for a year, and they would make the CFO the new CEO.

"We had a board dinner the night before my first board meeting, and everyone was getting along well. I asked the board member next to me in the course of getting to know him, 'Out of curiosity, why did you guys choose the CFO instead of the company's president for the CEO position?'

"He said, 'You know, that's a good question. We spent some time on it, but I'm not sure we looked at it from that angle.' So he turned to the guy to his left and engaged him with the same question. He, too, thought for a moment and said he wasn't sure precisely why. 'Well, we know [the CFO] well and we're sure he'll do a good job,' he said. 'But we didn't talk that much about alternatives.'

"I then explained: 'The reason I ask is because I think [the CFO] is going to be very important for the next six months,' because they were going to go through some transactions that we had been advocating. 'But after that, the person who's the president is really going to be a central player in a very critical role here.' Pretty soon the discussion spread to the whole table.

"I didn't go into the meeting planning to change this; it wasn't like the CFO was a poor choice. But as a result of that dinner, we decided as a board to reverse that decision." It was an awkward step for the company, of course, but the board came to a consensus that it would be beneficial to change course. That one question, posed in the spirit of congeniality but coming from a completely different point of view, had a huge positive impact. (Jerry Meyer confirmed this case example.)

It also helps if management is less defensive when an investor-nominated director is constructive and comes prepared with fresh perspectives or data. "They have to be satisfied that we're not a threat, and that we can actually be an ally to help them solve their problems, *and* maintain their positions," says Whitworth. But the investor-nominated director has to build that trust without appearing to create back-channels around other directors.

However, there is a caution, both for management and the board. While investor-nominated directors like Whitworth have proven to be constructive, not all are as helpful and skillful in adding to the board dynamics. Boards face greater difficulty when shareholders vote in a fast-buck investor whose interest is to alter the portfolio or sell the company quickly. This creates factions on the board that directors will simply have to learn to live with.

Working with Shareholder Proxies

Reaching out to shareholders also means working with shareholder advisory groups like RiskMetrics Group (of which Institutional Shareholder Services is part), the Corporate Library, and Governance Metrics. These proxy groups influence a large number of institutional investors, using frameworks to periodically rate the governance and compensation practices of companies. Many boards question the validity of their ratings, because the raters don't have much visibility into the factors that actually make a board effective. They primarily rate boards based on data available in public filings—are the CEO and chair roles separate, for example—and have no way to quantify whether the board's Lead Director and the group dynamics are effective.

Still, boards need to stop bellyaching and take the proxy groups very seriously. Major investors will often accept the proxy recommendations without question and factor the ratings into their investment decisions. Thus, boards need to pay attention to the ratings, both in positive and negative dimensions, however imperfect they are.

Even though they don't expose a board's group dynamics, the visible measures do matter. Should a director be present at every board meeting, for example? Of course she should. Can a CEO sit on nineteen boards and be effective on any of them? Unlikely. If RiskMetrics criticizes a board or a director, the board should carefully consider whether the point is valid.

If a board disagrees with a rating, the Lead Director or another appointed director can call to discuss it. The raters tend to have open doors; they will hear you out and may change their rating if your argument makes sense. RiskMetrics criticized me, for example, for my attendance at Tyco Electronics board meetings. When I called them to explain that I hadn't been elected to the board yet, they made the correction without argument. Of course, had I been on the board and missed those meetings, they would have been right.

The board has to be willing to listen to their criticisms and make changes. "I went with some of the board members to visit CalPERS and ISS, so there's been pretty active engagement on different aspects of executive compensation," says Jack Mollen, executive vice president for human resources of EMC Corp. "And they would tell us, for example, 'at the end of the day, the idea of having a tax gross-up is wrong.' So the compensation committee and the board would talk about it. And they were right. So we stopped it."

It's not easy to simply accept the recommendations of the proxy. Every change has consequences and the board has to make judgments about the trade-offs. In EMC's case, changing some aspects of their executive compensation could make the company less competitive in the market for talent if peer companies do not adopt similar proposals. In the end, however, the board decided that getting ahead of growing trends and governance standards was the right thing to do to protect the company's and the board's reputation.

Shareholder proxies are not perfect judges of a board's effectiveness, but accepting them is part of owning up.

Key Points

- Shareholder activism is here to stay. Boards need to change their psychology to see it as a constructive influence, not a nuisance.
- Boards must be prepared to communicate directly with shareholders when the situation warrants.
- Shareholders want the board to hear their concerns, but boards must be independent and sometimes push back.

- When investor-nominated directors are on the board, the group needs to work constructively to take advantage of their thinking.

- Boards must accept outside rating agencies, correct their errors, and not limit their self-improvement efforts to the agencies' narrow definitions of good governance.

About the Author

Ram Charan is a world-renowned adviser to corporate boards and business leaders, a best-selling author, and an award-winning teacher. He is known for his keen insights into business problems and his real-world practicality in solving them.

For nearly four decades, Ram has counseled some of the world's most successful business leaders on far-ranging issues, from corporate governance and building a leadership pipeline to pursuing organic growth. Most recently he has been deeply involved in helping boards and managements with the financial crisis and global economic slowdown.

Boards of directors were Ram's specialty and the subject of his doctoral thesis at Harvard Business School. He has deepened his knowledge of corporate governance ever since. For the past fifteen years he has been helping boards and CEOs deal with the practical challenges posed by rising societal expectations. He works with managements and boards to improve the functioning of the board and its contribution to the company. He assists boards in conducting board self-evaluations, peer reviews, and evaluations of the CEO. He helps key leaders (presiding or lead directors and committee chairs) make executive sessions productive and effective. Through retreats and facilitation, he helps managements and their boards get on the same page regarding company strategy, including its operational side. He also helps boards keep their composition in tune with the changing landscape through director succession planning and recruiting.

He himself is a director serving on three boards: Austin Industries, Tyco Electronics, and Emaar MGF in India. *Directorship* named him one of the top 100 directors of the year.

Ram, a prolific writer, is the author or coauthor of sixteen books, including *Boards That Deliver, Leadership in the Era of Economic Uncertainty, Know-How,* and *What the CEO Wants You to Know. Execution* was on the *New York Times'* best-seller list for nearly three years and has two million copies in print. Ram has contributed to lead articles in *Fortune, Harvard Business Review,* and many other publications.

Ram's interactive style and his real-world approach have made him a favorite among executive educators. He has taught for thirty consecutive years at GE's John F. Welch Leadership Center in Crotonville, New York, and Wharton's Insurance Institute. He has won best-teacher awards at Crotonville and Northwestern's Kellogg School of Management.

Ram has MBA and DBA degrees from Harvard Business School, where he graduated with high distinction and was a Baker Scholar. He was elected a Distinguished Fellow of the National Academy of Human Resources. He is based in Dallas, Texas.

Acknowledgments

As corporate boards face new challenges, I have been very lucky to learn from many great directors and business leaders who are owning up to their responsibilities and improving corporate governance at their companies. Many of the practices recommended in this book are the direct result of learning from them. I am especially grateful to the following people who carved out precious time to share with me their wisdom and experience: Frank Blake, Bonnie Hill, Brad Shaw, Dick Brown, Mike Campbell, Dennis Carey, Dave Calhoun, Richard Carrion, Bill Conaty, Charles Elson, J.P. Garnier, Dan Hesse, Janet Hill, Chad Holliday, Jeff Immelt, Brackett Denniston, Geoff Colvin, Lois Juliber, Andrea Jung, Roger Kenny, Jack Krol, John Luke, John Lynch, Bill McCracken, J.P. Millon, Rich Noll, Jerry Meyer, Frank Placenti, Jim Robinson, Hellene Runtagh, Tom Neff, Joe Tucci, Jack Mollen, Kevin Close, Bob Weissman, and Ralph Whitworth. I also want to acknowledge the learning and support from my director colleagues at Tyco Electronics, Austin Industries, and Emaar MGF, who have been generous with their time and insights and allowed me to test some of the ideas presented here: Ron Gafford, Paul Hill, James Andoga, Barry Babyak, David Walls, Rhys Best, David Biegler, Frederick Hegi, James Hoak, Dorothy Collins Weaver, Pierre Brondeau, Juergen Gromer, Robert Hernandez, Thomas Lynch, Daniel Phelan, Frederic Poses, Lawrence Smith, Paula Sneed, David Steiner, Sandra Wijnberg, and V.K. Gomber. It is a privilege to serve with them.

This book would not have been possible without the fantastic editorial contributions of Larry Yu and Geri Willigan, who turned the learning into clear, succinct prose that is respectful of readers' time and intelligence. I wish to thank them and John Joyce, who provided useful inputs along the way. A number of people at Jossey-Bass—in particular, Susan Williams, Byron Schneider, Rob Brandt, and Mark Karmendy—provided excellent help in taking the book from concept to a high-quality final product.

There is no such thing as "business as usual" in my Dallas office, yet Cynthia Burr, Karen Baker, and Carol Davis make it seem as though there is. I am very grateful to their magical ability to keep me and my projects on track.

Last, I am grateful to every director and business leader who takes his or her responsibility seriously, continuously tries to learn and improve, and is willing to help others do the same. Their efforts give me confidence that there is a positive way forward not just for their companies but also for society as a whole, even in these uncertain times.

Ram Charan
January 2009

Index